UNDERSTANDING AND LOVING A PERSON WITH

BORDERLINE PERSONALITY DISORDER

UNDERSTANDING AND LOVING A PERSON WITH

BORDERLINE PERSONALITY DISORDER

*Biblical and Practical Wisdom
to Build Empathy, Preserve Boundaries,
and Show Compassion*

STEPHEN ARTERBURN, M.Ed.
AND ROBERT WISE, Ph.D.

David C Cook®
transforming lives together

UNDERSTANDING AND LOVING A PERSON WITH
BORDERLINE PERSONALITY DISORDER
Published by David C Cook
4050 Lee Vance Drive
Colorado Springs, CO 80918 U.S.A.

David C Cook U.K., Kingsway Communications
Eastbourne, East Sussex BN23 6NT, England

The graphic circle C logo is a registered trademark of David C Cook.

The website addresses recommended throughout this book are offered as a
resource to you. These websites are not intended in any way to be or imply an
endorsement on the part of David C Cook, nor do we vouch for their content.

Details in some stories have been changed to protect the identities of the persons involved.

Unless otherwise noted, all Scripture quotations are taken from
the New King James Version®. Copyright © 1982 by Thomas Nelson. Used by
permission. All rights reserved; ESV are taken from the ESV® Bible (The Holy Bible,
English Standard Version®), copyright © 2001 by Crossway, a publishing ministry
of Good News Publishers. Used by permission. All rights reserved; NASB are taken
from the New American Standard Bible®, copyright © 1960, 1995 by The Lock-
man Foundation. Used by permission. (www.Lockman.org); RSV are taken from
are taken from the Revised Standard Version of the Bible, copyright 1952 [2nd
edition, 1971] by the Division of Christian Education of the National Council
of the Churches of Christ in the USA. Used by permission. All rights reserved.

LCCN 2017935675
ISBN 978-0-7814-1489-0
eISBN 978-1-4347-1235-6

© 2017 Stephen Arterburn
The Author is represented by and this book is published in association with the
literary agency of WordServe Literary Group, Ltd., www.wordserveliterary.com.

Cover Design: Amy Konyndyk
Cover Photo: Getty Images

Printed in the United States of America
First Edition 2017

1 2 3 4 5 6 7 8 9 10

072817

Contents

Introduction

Welcome to the Arterburn Wellness Series. This is one of several books in the series that focuses on major difficulties we all face in relationships. I hope you and others who find their way to this series develop a better understanding of the people you care about, their problems, and your long-term responses to them.

The fact that you are reading this book means that you are most likely in a relationship with someone possessing one of the most difficult disorders—so difficult that for decades professionals believed there was no hope for someone with borderline personality disorder (BPD). Continue to read and you will discover that hope exists.

And let me say something right away about the danger of labels if your loved one has not been diagnosed: to automatically put this particular label on someone, without firm proof and understanding of the disorder, is not your best strategy. He or she may indeed have BPD, but don't jump to that conclusion just yet. It's a puzzling disorder, mostly because of the way a person with BPD can make you feel.

The person can be fascinating, attractive, engaging, and fun. At the same time, you could add unpredictable, mind-boggling, destructive, suicidal, and dangerous. These are all accurate descriptions of the same person.

For centuries, the most common and also most accurate descriptor was the word *confusing*. This disorder produces a walking contradiction. Your relationship can start as instant best friendship, and then it can morph and flip-flop until all of a sudden this same person becomes your worst enemy.

When someone with this disorder seeks help, he or she will often cause confusion for the helper. In decades past, professionals thought the individual might be psychotic, but research also has put a *neurotic* label on it. The truth is, BPD is right on the border between neurosis and psychosis. The border is where the person plays out his or her survival techniques. So the term *borderline* is now used to describe the person and the disorder.

In this book, you will go back in time or, more accurately, back to the future—not in a DeLorean with an old guy named Doc Brown but back to the early days of childhood, when a person's natural development is supposed to be taking place. It's there that this challenging future got its start. So if you don't know about your loved one's childhood, it will be difficult to develop the compassion needed to stay sane while you engage in a helpful relationship with him or her.

In the childhood of a person with BPD, there was often severe abuse. Or perhaps something more difficult to understand, such as emotional incest from a person of trust. Most likely, one relationship or more was marked by deep statements or acts of love, care, and concern and often abandonment, rejection, and disconnection from that very same person.

These experiences result in a person—possibly your loved one with BPD—living life full of fear. People with BPD do not fully grasp how their actions affect others, mainly because they haven't fully processed how they were treated. They might think they crave deep relationships and intimate connections, but those might be the only ways they have found to assure themselves that people won't abandon them. They might find it difficult to even give a glance to the reality that if they develop intimate connections, they may be unable to maintain them. So they instinctively find some very dramatic ways to break from such connections.

The very real pain and confusion they go through are paralleled by your own. You fear for their lives and sometimes—maybe a lot of times—you fear they may stay alive.

How do I know these traits?

Because all my life, my own fragile, people-pleasing ego has been attracted to all that is wonderful and good about the person with borderline personality disorder. I even coauthored a book with David A. Stoop titled *When Someone You Love Is Someone You Hate.*

I have been driving with a BPD person in my car when the only thing keeping the person from not jumping out onto the pavement while going fifty miles per hour was my grip on his arm. The next day, he acted as if the incident had never happened. I have walked into the house of a woman with BPD who had butcher knives on the floor as the result of a staged break-in from a supposedly deadly stalker that would require me to protect this innocent victim. It was all concocted to draw me in. I would later learn from an old boyfriend of hers that I had been duped. He asked me, "Has she pulled the 'fake break-in by a stalker with butcher knives on the floor' stunt she pulled on me?" After I picked up my jaw from the floor, I did not run from her; I dove right in, wanting to fix her ... or at least do all I could to help her.

So I hope you see that I understand your pain, frustration, and feelings of powerlessness to make things better.

But there are things you *can* do to make things better—for you and the person you love. I know you will find those things in this book by Robert Wise. Professionals have learned so much in the past few years that this disorder, which was once thought to be hopeless, is now something that can be understood, managed, and yes, even changed.

You will find all that here, and my prayer for you is that when you have finished reading, you will be filled with hope for yourself, the one you love, and the relationship you have forged together.

—Stephen Arterburn

CHAPTER ONE

Blindsided!

Do any of these sound like experiences you've lived through with someone you love?

- You worry that what you say may be twisted and taken out of context.
- You've become the target for intense and sometimes violent responses to innocent questions or simple inquiries.
- The other person seems to be denying what you know is reality, and it makes you feel crazy.
- The significant other in your life inevitably puts you down and abruptly hits you from out of nowhere.
- This important person in your life accuses you of irresponsible behavior, sexual misconduct, lies, or antagonism when you know these charges are not true.

If these are just the beginning of what you have been worrying about and struggling with, then this book will help you.

An Unexpected Visit

Alice Jones had been around the church for almost a month. The first Sunday she attended, Alice was overwhelmingly enthusiastic about what the services had meant to her that day. She particularly thanked me for how I had helped her. Since that time, I had seen her around the building several times. She had never failed to express her appreciation. When she showed up in my office one afternoon a few weeks later, I expected another round of applause.

Was I wrong!

"I was talking with one of your members," Alice began. "She wasn't happy."

"Oh," I said, "there's a problem?"

"Seems you don't give your members much of your personal attention," Alice said as her smile disappeared and her eyes narrowed. "Some of your folks feel left out."

I blinked and tried to let my mind catch up with what my ears were hearing. Nothing clicked. I wasn't connecting with anything she was saying.

"May I sit down?" Alice asked as she dropped into the chair before I could answer. "It seems like you are so caught up in your own ideas that you don't pay much attention to people's problems."

"Wait a minute," I said, mystified. "I've never had anyone complain about me being indifferent. On the contrary, most people would say I'm always concerned."

"Well, you don't show it."

"What are you suggesting?" I asked, now feeling defensive.

"Take me, for instance. I've been here for a number of weeks, and we've never sat down and had a personal conversation."

"I really am not tracking with you, Alice."

"See! That's just it!" Her voice became shrill. "You don't get it. Let me tell you a thing or two. I'm not going to put up with being treated indifferently. You aren't going to use me as your punching bag!" She was now on the verge of yelling. "Get somebody else to treat like a dog. I'm out of here!" Alice stomped out of the room and slammed the door.

I don't use this word often, but I was most definitely *thunderstruck.*

Hit by Lightning

If you have thought you had a relationship with someone only to be suddenly smacked in the head for some unknown reason, this book is for you. If you've been completely unable to comprehend something disturbing that happened with someone you thought was your friend, you've come to the right place. Did you ever have a cordial friendship and then suddenly the individual attacked, exploded, screamed, or accused you? Then you know how it feels to be run over by someone who might have BPD.

I've known people who thought they married their perfect matches only to discover that their mates were not who they appeared to be. It's true that everyone has to make adjustments in a marriage as he or she gets to know the other person in depth, but the problems with a loved one with BPD usually demand far more than compromises and accommodation. The other person proves to be difficult, harsh, and even treacherous. How can people misread one another so much?

Some years ago, Susan came to my office for counseling. George, the man she had married, had turned into a "control freak." Every dime she spent had to go through her husband's hands. He demanded she keep the house in a certain order. He controlled their children as if they were horses with bits in their mouths. George was always on Susan's case and condemned everything she did.

During the counseling process, George suddenly lost all interest in his wife and began an affair with another woman. After a confrontation with Susan one evening, he jumped on his motorcycle and went speeding down the highway. George missed a sharp turn and went flying into a freshly plowed field. A short while later, he died.

Even though George was gone, Susan struggled to understand what had gone wrong. Was it her fault? Why had this man been so impossible? Why did she feel so run over all the time?

The goal of this book is twofold. First, it will help people like Susan—and perhaps you—unravel the mystery of why these people you love are so difficult and unpredictable. You will be able to recognize a borderline personality, and you will be in a better position to respond. Second, information is power, and this book will empower you not only to understand but perhaps also to empathize with people with BPD. This won't come naturally. People with BPD are not always loveable or easy to figure out.

We are going to examine in depth how troubled personalities operate. Although people with BPD push others to the edge, it is possible to develop empathy and insight that can lead to change. Hopefully, you will even become an agent for renewal and healing.

Not only will you discover how to understand their behavior, but you will learn to protect yourself, make your interactions with them more positive, and hopefully love them.

Don't worry if you feel alone. Help is on the way.

Undependable

A counselor friend of mine told me about the Allan family, whom he'd known for a number of years. The mother and father had both been in and out of trouble many times. Drugs were no small part of their conflicts. Various relatives were raising their three children. Sadly, this arrangement had not worked out well for the kids.

Their youngest son, Jack, loved his mother and father despite how they treated him. Unfortunately, Jack couldn't keep out of trouble. By the time he had become an adult, Jack had served a short prison term. Because my friend had helped the family, Jack turned to him for counseling advice.

Jack was immediately enthusiastic. He thought my friend could be his mentor and help him straighten out his life. Jack particularly wanted help with his finances. Jack believed my friend's insights on investing could help him turn his life around and enable him to become a success.

Over the course of a month, they had several intense conversations, and then Jack made no further contact. After several weeks, my friend tried to find out what had become of Jack. Finally, he discovered that Jack had spontaneously left town and moved to Canada. He was now working as a mechanic in Calgary, Alberta. When he finally got Jack on the phone, Jack laughed and said he was playing with some children at the moment and would call back later. But my friend never heard from Jack again.

When someone abruptly drops us, treats us badly, or becomes erratic for no good reason, we are naturally bewildered. What did *we* do wrong? How could this have happened? Where did *we* miss the boat? The natural assumption is that *we* are somehow at fault. Self-blame is unavoidable when we have no explanation for someone's erratic behavior. One of the most difficult aspects of working with a troubled person is that conscientious people tend to blame themselves for what went wrong. We struggle to understand what we said or did that caused the problem. We need to know why. We think it's time to stop and recognize we've made a wrong turn.

I want to convince you of one thing before we go any further. Some relationships go sideways, and it *might not be your fault* in the least.

This book will give you insight when …

- the other person's behavior is erratic and unpredictable.
- you feel responsible but know it can't be your fault.
- the other person makes you feel crazy.
- the other person's responses are not appropriate for the situation.
- you have been deceived.
- a timid person turns into a lion.
- you can't figure out what went wrong.

This short list might be the tip of the iceberg when you are trying to understand and love people with BPD. Why? Their odd behaviors are not only unexpected but usually completely out of order. Their behavior leaves you dumbfounded nearly every time. You have become a victim.

You might feel like giving up, but don't throw up your hands quite yet. You have to turn over every rock as you try to understand how these personalities function. Usually damaged emotions produce such unexpected behavior. People with BPD have deeper motivations behind what they do and what they say—motivations you never would have dreamed of.

Behavioral Knots

Loved ones with BPD have knots in their brains and emotions they haven't figured out how to untie. While the irrationality of their behavior seems obvious—sometimes even offensive—to us, it seems quite normal to them. They lack inner mirrors to see themselves as their victims see them. Their confusion comes across as narcissistic and self-absorbed.

What makes them so problematic is that they can still maintain some degree of concern for others. If someone is particularly close to them, they are able to respond with kindness. However, what makes them difficult to handle is that they suddenly shut down the positive side of their personalities and become completely negative. Relating to people with BPD has often been called "crazy making." People with BPD can be high spirited and positive one day and indifferent the next.

Reason to Hope

Whether difficult or totally self-absorbed, BPD types have a history that can equip us to understand them. We can learn how to deal with their behavior.

Although they generally leave us angry and frustrated, good reasons exist for feeling sorry for them and wanting to help them. In the following chapters, we will explore what we can do to make a difference. But first, let's take a ten-thousand-foot view of this disorder and look at it a bit more clinically. It's more common than you think.

During my years as a pastor, I encountered the same problem again and again. I struggled with both men and women as they tried to straighten out relationships that were highly important to them, but the significant other wouldn't seem to budge. During my years studying psychotherapy in graduate school, I attempted to understand how borderline personalities function and what can be done to help them. In the following chapters, I will take you with me on this journey to make sense of what feels like nonsense. My objective is to help both you and the troubled person. I don't want you to be a victim again.

I'm sure you've felt alone many times, but that's no longer the case. I am with you!

CHAPTER TWO

Tension and Turmoil

Mark seemed like the world's nicest guy. He came to our singles group looking for acceptance after a failed marriage. When asked, Mark described how his uncompromising, demanding ex-wife nearly drove him over the cliff. He rambled often and considered himself a volunteer in the group. Mark was glad to be there to help anyone he could.

Everyone was encouraged when Mark developed a relationship with Ann. Ann had gone through a painful divorce when her husband left immediately after the birth of their daughter. Ann's small daughter, Mary, had been born with a birth defect and mental limitations. Ann's ex-husband couldn't tolerate a defective child. But Mark wasn't put off by any of these problems and showed affectionate attention to little Mary. The future appeared bright for Ann. In a short time, Mark asked her to marry him, promising to care for Mary.

A couple of months after the wedding, I noticed Ann's usual happy disposition had faded. She didn't smile as much as she once did. Because little Mary had her ups and downs, I thought the child might be going through some difficult moments that depressed Ann. I didn't say anything.

Time went by, and several people remarked that Mark had become rather demanding. He was responsible for keeping the church kitchen in good order, and when people didn't follow his rules, Mark snapped at them.

Several people became angry and let me know.

Six months later, Ann came to my office and nearly exploded with anger and frustration. While another divorce was the last thing she wanted, Ann couldn't live with Mark anymore. He had laid out a set of rules that Ann was to follow—and if she didn't, all hell broke loose. Kitchen chairs had to be placed in an exact way around the table. Silverware and napkins had to be put in the "correct position" (his description) next to the plates. Mark told her how to dress and demanded to know where she was every second of the day.

Ann's list of complaints went on and on. Because I knew about Mark's run-ins around the church, I knew Ann wasn't exaggerating. We had all been deceived by a BPD person who wore a smiling mask. When he took it off, everyone who crossed Mark's path paid a price.

Where Are We Going?

In this chapter, I will define why people like Mark are a problem. We want to take an analytical look at their behavior and get a more definite understanding of what is going on.

Clinical psychology has a number of categories that describe personality disorders as typified by people like Mark. It helps to know that the troubling individuals might have an emotional condition that causes them to be so erratic. A personality disorder is generally what it's called when someone thinks about himself or herself in a way that constantly causes problems in everyday relationships. Often a professional can help clarify the nature of the problem. Frequently, a troubled person may have several overlapping difficulties. Let's look at some of the possibilities that might come under the same heading as a borderline personality. The following categories will give you a general idea of what is going on inside people like Mark. Don't worry about becoming a diagnostician. I merely want you to have a working knowledge of how some personality disorders have close cousins. Insight will be important. Recognizing deviant behaviors will help keep you from being victimized. You will be able to spot a problem before the other person drops a bomb on you. Here are some examples of different troubled personalities.

Borderline Personality Disorder

Persons with this diagnosis generally have difficulty with interpersonal relationships. Their self-image is as full of holes as Swiss cheese. They usually cause you to feel they have a piece missing. They have deep-seated fears of abandonment. While they might first conceal the problem, emotional instability eventually surfaces. They often display impulsive behavior. They can make a dramatic shift from seeing someone as a hero to castigating him or her as a villain.

You might be wondering why you haven't heard of borderline personality disorder before. That's because this is a more recently recognized category of behavior. In the first half of the twentieth century, researchers considered these problems to be halfway between neurosis and psychosis, and that's where the name *borderline* came from. In the 1970s, they discarded that concept, but the name stayed. The concern not to create a stigmatizing label kept usage of the term reserved to some extent.[1]

At this point, hard statistics on the number of people with BPD in the general population are unavailable. However, 70 percent of those diagnosed are female. Sexual abuse appears in 40 to 70 percent of the cases. Community clinics report that 11 to 20 percent of their inpatients fall into this category. Seventy-five percent of people with BPD had a history of self-harm.[2] In other words, BPD persons exist in a significant number. Today, the counseling and psychiatric communities take this problem very seriously. However, clients are generally resistant to recognize their problem. They feel "somebody" has done something to them; therefore, they don't think they need therapeutic help. Moreover, they often tend to drop out of counseling and return to their old patterns of behavior. In fact, many counselors won't even begin therapy with a BPD individual because the process is long and the treatment so difficult to predict.

Avoidant Personality Disorder

Usually shy and easily offended, these people feel they are not as good as others. They do not open up well to romantic relationships and try to avoid employment that forces them to be in contact with others. They appear to be loners. Avoidance types disappear in a group and are not good at self-promotion at the office or on the job.

When they explain what bothers them, avoidance types blow events and situations out of proportion. They have a jaundiced eye when they look at difficult situations that involved them. They tend to feel they are victims or marginalized. Many adults in this category are a bit more self-aware of their issues than are borderline personalities.

Antisocial Personality Disorder

Get ready for manipulation when you run into one of these people.

Antisocial types tend to perform criminal acts. They lie, steal, explode, violate other people's space, get angry, and have no regrets about any of these behaviors. Breaking the law is as easy as getting up in the morning. In today's world, they often end up as substance abusers. One of the most consistent and difficult problems with antisocial types is that they use people for their own benefit.

Obsessive-Compulsive Personality Disorder

These folks absolutely follow the rules ... *all* the rules. Their goal is to be perfect, and they avoid anything that might tarnish this objective. One of the most difficult problems in reacting to their behavior is that they are incapable of being flexible. Usually, they are not generous. They do not demonstrate affection and can seem distant. When they get into a profession, they become obsessed with their work and might work at the office long after everyone else is gone.

Narcissistic Personality Disorder

An entire book in this series will cover this subject, but generally, narcissists have a pattern of grandiosity and an exaggerated sense of self-importance. They have little empathy and focus almost entirely on themselves. They routinely overestimate their abilities, and they are inclined to overstate their accomplishments. Their relationships tend to reflect their conviction that only the upper class, the talented, are worthy of a relationship with them. Often they feel others are envious of them. Because they need and expect admiration, their demands can irritate.

Dependent Personality Disorder

Dependent types lean on everyone around them to meet their physical and emotional needs. They have a hard time making independent decisions and don't want to be left alone. They often worry about being abandoned and fret over what other people think of them. Disapproval can throw them for a loop. Generally, they struggle with criticism. Dependent people are often described as "clinging vine" types.

Histrionic Personality Disorder

These folks come loaded with excessive emotion. They know how to get attention through all sorts of demonstrative behaviors. If they are not the center of attention, they are uneasy. Histrionics major in drama, making up stories, creating scenes, and demanding the spotlight. They express strong opinions with a dramatic flair. They are good at showing up with gifts and flattery, and they like to play that old game, "Let's talk about how great I am." They are known to exhibit provocative behavior and can be sexually seductive.

Get the Picture?

Can you discern any common root problems that all these personality disorders share? Do you see similar issues? Here are some of the ways they tie together.

While it might be difficult to see at the outset, weakness is at the bottom of BPD behavior. Usually, their odd way of relating feels like an imposition of their power, but as we can now see from these descriptions, low self-esteem is a major issue. At the very least, with this insight, people like Ann can begin to understand the conflicts that arise out of the other person's problems. Because all of us tend to assume we did something wrong when there's an issue, getting the right perspective is an essential starting point to staying balanced. A second look reveals that all these groups share the basic problem of feeling weak or inadequate. These people may scream at you, but behind the scenes, they feel highly inadequate.

Most people with a flexible personality can adapt to unexpected situations and adjust to other people. But folks with personality disorders are stuck in their rigid ways of reacting. They may become impulsive or retreat, and their behavior becomes chronic. Because they don't understand themselves, we have to reach out and help them discover a larger vision of what they can become.

Where does all this difficulty and tension come from? Most psychologists agree that the American family has exacerbated the problem. With more than half of all marriages ending in divorce, many kids are set adrift to figure life out as best they can. In their earliest years, a defect is created in their personalities, and that's where the trouble begins.[3]

If a child is not raised by at least one caring mother or father—both being preferable—the child is often not emotionally prepared for life. In the last fifty years, the rate of teenagers who became addicted to drugs or committed suicide increased dramatically. Not having a constructive father or mother leaves a void in the child's personality. The child is set adrift and then flounders during adolescence.

While we can confidently say that these souls, precious both to God and to those who love them, are in many ways victims of their pasts, we have to arm ourselves with knowledge so we do not become their victims. Sadly, hurting people *do* hurt others, and those with BPD transfer their own pain to innocent people to make themselves feel better … but they truly devastate those caught in their wake.

This book is a good starting point to help you understand how to respond as well as how to recognize the importance of creating a better environment for love and understanding.

Here are some key questions for you (or your loved one) to ponder in attempting to identify the nature and source of the tension and turmoil. A borderline person might also have some of the traits of narcissistic, obsessive-compulsive, or antisocial personalities. The expression of their problems might come out in any of these categories. I have adapted the following key questions from Quizscope.com for your consideration. Take a careful look.

Identifying Troublesome People

- Do they have unstable and intense relationships with alternating extremes of love and hate? If so, they likely have nasty fights with family and friends—and then suddenly it's as if the altercation never happened.
- Do they seem to have an unstable self-image or a poor sense of self? If so, you'll notice their self-worth is a problem. They probably lack an enduring awareness of who they are.

- Have you observed impulsive, self-destructive behavior? If so, you'll likely also see that illegal drug usage is common, as is unprotected sex. They tend to act out in ways that are completely contrary to their own best interests.
- Have you observed self-mutilation or ever heard them express suicidal thoughts? Cut marks on the arms or hands are important clues that something is wrong. You must take their expressions of self-negation seriously.
- Even when there is no real threat, do they periodically make frantic efforts to avoid what they consider abandonment? You'll notice they'll often do anything to avoid being alone.
- Do they have frequent, intense mood swings or emotionally overreact? Like race cars, they can go from calm to furious in a split second; their anger can last for an hour or perhaps days.
- Do they have chronic feelings of emptiness, and nothing fills the void? They may feel this vacant space all the time. It's as if their gas gauge is stuck on empty.
- Have you seen inappropriate, intense anger or watched them struggle to control their anger? It truly makes no difference where they are or who's around; everyone can get whacked by their anger.
- Do they ever have temporary episodes of paranoia or lose contact with reality? Sometimes they may feel as if they're having an "out-of-body" experience.

What Did You Find?

Did these categories and questions help you discover some clues about what might be going on with the difficult people in your world? Do any of these descriptions line up with your suspicions? Remember that some people are a combination of these categories and could have behavior that fits several of these descriptions. When people of faith try to follow the admonition to "love one another," they need all the help they can find to understand why the struggle to show affection can be so difficult.

Unfortunately, no one has come up with a personality test to definitely indicate diagnostically that a person has a borderline personality. The line is blurry because BPD is often confused with other problems, such as bipolar disorder or depression, that can co-occur with BPD. A qualified mental health professional can provide an accurate assessment.[4] However, the foregoing questions will give you some strong hints.

• •

Remember:
Don't assume a confrontation is all *your* fault!

• •

CHAPTER THREE

Finding Solid Ground When the Earth Shakes

Bob had one fear: losing love.

Only after significant counseling did he begin to recognize what happened to him when he was threatened. As a child, he sensed when a teacher didn't seem to particularly like him. Bob would suddenly become extremely angry to the extent that the teacher could not control him. Sometimes the school would call his parents to attempt to get him back in order.

As Bob matured, his anger problem didn't cool down. Under the right circumstances, he could become uncontrollably explosive. Several times, he nearly got fired at the office because of an outburst. Through counseling, Bob discovered that his anger was only a cover for his fear. The truth was that he was afraid no one loved him. Because he didn't know how to handle his anxiety, he also could not control his anger. With time, he began to understand his dread of not being loved. Positive changes began to develop.

If Bob was a next-door neighbor or personal friend, could we show him the love he needed? That's the challenge we face with people with BPD. They need the love that they often resist.

We can get a handle on stability when we identify the underlying psychological problems of troublesome people. Borderline persons often leave us feeling perplexed. When our motives have been positive, we generally assume we have done something to cause the problem. Knowledge of the causes clarifies the situation and releases us from undeserved responsibility.

Everyone needs help in learning how to maintain stability. We need to discover firm footing when it feels like the room is becoming earthquake central. Having someone shout in our faces leaves us in shock—with our hearts pounding, adrenalin pumping, palms sweating, and consciences working overtime. What in heaven's name did we do to create such an outburst?

Screaming Sarah

Sarah had always been a large woman, but being overweight wasn't the problem. Friends and acquaintances soon learned how temperamental Sarah could be. After one of her screaming explosions, they often drifted away to avoid another anger assault. I first met Sarah after her divorce.

"I want to help around the church," Sarah said. "I need new stability after what I've been through." She rolled her eyes.

"How would you feel about working in our kitchen?" I suggested. "Sounds great," Sarah said. "I love working around my kitchen at home. What do you want me to do?"

"People sometimes use dishes and leave them out," I said. "After our all-church dinners, someone must straighten up the area and make sure the kitchen is left in order."

"Perfect! When do you want me to start?"

"Right now is fine."

"Good. Consider your problems solved. The kitchen is taken care of."

As time went by, I learned more than I wanted to know about Sarah's divorce. Her former husband sounded like a decent guy running for cover. Church members related that her fights with her ex had been so bad, he was planning to leave the state to get away from her. I tried to stay above the noise, but eventually Sarah's anger caused a problem for the church: Sarah had arbitrarily put padlocks on all the kitchen cabinets.

"We really have a problem," Jerry the janitor told me. "You can't get in the cabinets when you need a glass or some silverware."

"Why in the world were they locked in the first place?" I asked.

"I heard that Sarah got into an argument with somebody about dishes being left in the sink, and she just went out and bought locks. She told a lady in the church that she wouldn't give anyone the key."

"We can't have that," I said. "She didn't talk with me and certainly not the church board. Can you take the locks off?"

"Sure," Jerry said, "I've got a heavy-duty bolt cutter that will do the trick. Won't take me long." He walked out.

I went back to work in my office. The afternoon was fleeting, and I needed to finish up before five o'clock if possible. Fifteen minutes later, the secretary came running into my office.

"Pastor, we've got a war going on in the kitchen! Jerry needs your help."

I hurried after her. Halfway down the hall, I could hear shouting. When I reached the kitchen, I saw that Sarah had Jerry cornered, and she was screaming at the top of her lungs.

"How dare you sneak in here and destroy *my* locks! I put those on to keep the uninvited out of the shelves. And that means you!" She shook her finger in his face.

"Wait a minute," I intervened. "Sarah, you didn't ask anyone about locking up those doors."

She whirled around with fire flashing in her eyes. "The kitchen is my property," she hissed. "You gave me control of this room."

"No, I asked you to help us. The kitchen has to be open to everyone."

Sarah's eyes narrowed. "So now you're on Jerry's side?"

"I'm not on anyone's side. I'm simply saying we all need access to the kitchen, and locked doors prohibit that."

Sarah inhaled a deep breath like a dragon about to breathe fire. "You men are all alike." She slammed her fist down on the countertop. "To hell with you! I'm not putting up with this abuse any longer." Sarah grabbed her purse, pushed the secretary aside, and stomped out of the building.

We never saw her again.

We can learn from Sarah's explosion. Persons with BPD can reverse field before we even know the ball was snapped. When this occurs, don't discount their sudden change as a misunderstanding on your part. In addition, their anger may come in from left field.

● ●

Don't be surprised by how extreme a person with BPD can be!

● ●

The Four Symptoms of BPD

Borderline personality disorder has four basic symptoms. Remembering these categories can help you recognize where the conflict comes from and what may be creating the confrontation.

1. *Impaired emotional control.* People with BPD have poorly regulated emotional responses. When they become angry, they can change quickly from calm to chaotic. If their reaction is excessive and seems out of control, that is a sign of the borderline problem.

2. *Harmful impulsivity.* They can fly off the handle or turn around and deplete their bank accounts with a shopping spree. People with BPD often engage in self-harm, such as cutting. They can be sexually indiscreet or abruptly drink too much. Don't be confused by their sudden actions.

3. *Impaired perceptions and reasoning.* An unstable self-image and a poor sense of identity are common symptoms, so they might not reason well. They can tend toward suspiciousness and misperceptions. Don't be surprised if your reasoning with them goes nowhere.

4. *Disrupted relationships.* People with BPD tend to have tumultuous relationships that drive others away. Their confrontations are often caused by excessive anger, fear of abandonment, or simply the desire to run. When you see people with BPD destroying important relationships, recognize that they might have no perspective on what they are doing or why they are doing it.[1]

First Aid: Diagnosis

When these altercations occur, the injured need first aid for their wounded egos. Some collisions can take years to heal. Decades later, people might still be emotionally limping. A few immediate responses can help them stay on their feet and avoid long-term resentments. Here are some clues that can help. Consider these questions.

1. What's Going on Internally with This Person?

In Sarah's case, she was a control freak. She had a compulsive need to keep everything under her thumb. She went berserk when the locks were cut off because she was no longer in the driver's seat.

Control is a major issue for many people with BPD. Fear and a dread of possible chaos hide underneath their shrill tones. As long as they have their hands on the control switch, they are secure. However, they fear that loss of domination will leave them at the mercy of their attackers (and that includes anyone who disagrees with them for any reason).[2]

Consider the difference if I had had the presence of mind to say, "Sarah, you can still have authority and can direct the kitchen without locking the cabinets. No one doubts your judgment, but we need uninhibited access to the dishes." The chances are good that she would have cooled off enough to listen and something constructive might have been worked out.

* *

Before you get swept up in the conflict, mentally take a step back and ask yourself, "What's really going on? Am I being manipulated? What is this person *actually* acting out?"

* *

2. Is Control an Issue?

Sarah was far more concerned with *appearing to be in control* than with what she privately felt. Appearance is everything for the Sarahs of the world. Whether they recognize it or not, image is paramount to these types.

Characteristics such as integrity, understanding, insight, or the feelings of others are not on their radar screen. Self-promotion to keep the image of control intact is what counts.

Unfortunately, these persons have a carryover problem from their earliest years. They never developed a true sense of themselves.

Struggling with issues that circulated around the center of their personalities like a rampant whirlpool, they did not evolve constructive objectives for a well-balanced life. They have little sense of how others are affected by their actions. Generally speaking, emptiness is at the center of their emotions. To cover these deficits, they struggle to project the right image and stay on top of all emotional situations. They must stay in control.[3]

- -

Ask yourself, "Who is in control in an emotional encounter?" Remember: *It's not them.*

- -

3. What Type of Image Is This Person Trying to Convey?

Since keeping the right persona in place is important to those with BPD, we should ask ourselves what they are actually trying to demonstrate when they go off like a rocket. Strength? Superiority? Their all-knowing character? Competence? Their ability to frighten us? While the list could be long, a hard second look will generally give us clues as to what is going on.

Sarah clearly wanted to portray herself as someone in charge. She probably did the same with her husband. Without realizing her problem, Jerry and I circumvented her attempts to appear as the top dog.

A friend of mine once ended up in a power struggle with an oil and gas lawyer over a budget. Since my friend didn't operate the church on the basis of wealth or prestige, he overlooked the lawyer, which created a big problem. The lawyer imagined himself as the top dog, but my friend missed the signals. Later, the lawyer nearly destroyed the church in his effort to impress the congregation with his significance.

BPD people can be successful, but they are still as troublesome as ever.

* *

Remember to consider what image the person is trying to project.

* *

4. What Values Is the Person Willing to Jettison in the Conflict?

Often people with BPD talk or operate in a mechanical way. Difficult people can make you feel like you are talking to a wall. While you might assume people have or want relationships with long-term meaning, difficult people generally don't.

Sarah *said* she wanted meaningful involvement, but she *meant* she wanted to be in control of something. Friendly relationships weren't important to her. Sarah was willing to jettison personal relationships to stay in charge.

Such people are difficult because of their indifference. However, if you can identify some characteristics that the individual disregards, you will have a better sense of how to handle the situation. For example, my friend thought the lawyer was someone who also cared about people, failing to realize that all relationships that didn't serve his purposes were expendable. The lawyer has been through three divorces, and my friend is still not sure if he's recognized the value of relationships yet.

When you are caught in a conflict, it can be difficult to recognize what is missing. However, after you've had time to step back and think it over, you might be able to identify the missing piece in the puzzle. At the least, you will be ready to understand the person better the next time there is a conflict.

. . . .

Keep asking yourself, "What values are they dismissing?"

. . . .

5. How Can I Stay Balanced?

Whether we like it or not, the emotional upheaval within the person with BPD shapes our responses. Their angry explosions hit us like bombshells and make us feel disoriented. When people scream and shout in our faces, we become emotionally disjointed, and we can't help but feel like our gears have been stripped. Before the personal assault comes, it's important to consider how to stay in balance.[4]

Stability demands emotional distance from the heated conversation. If we get sucked into the dynamics of discord, we can't stay on an even keel. Before we make any response, a buzzer needs to go off in our heads that tells us to mentally step back. Even if we need to close our eyes for a moment, we must disconnect ourselves from the immediate upheaval.

High-strung people leave a trail of human debris behind them because their victims get caught up in the passionate energy released in their volcanic eruptions. The victims lose sight of the fact that the person with BPD directed, controlled, and manipulated these vehement attacks. Like an unseen riptide that drags a person to the bottom, the victim never saw what was coming until it was too late.

You need mental reminders until your responses become second nature. For example, if you anticipate walking into a problematic situation, you can keep a small note card in your pocket or purse that you can periodically review to remind yourself how to respond. You must keep an emotional distance when a person with BPD explodes, and remembering the correct response can help you maintain stability.

• •

Remind yourself to keep an emotional distance when you encounter the difficult person.

• •

Our Job

When the emotional wars start, we naturally want to fight back, but that will only complicate matters. If we want to be constructive, then we must attempt to get the BPD person back in touch with his humanity. He will only be able to get out of attack mode by recognizing values other than those he is acting out. When the person feels compassion, gentleness, warmth, or kindness, his reactions can rise to a higher level.

For years, I read Charles Dickens's *A Christmas Carol,* impersonating Ebenezer Scrooge. Everyone loved to sit back and listen to the tale of a transformed life. When I reached the end of the story and Ebenezer Scrooge emerged a new, happy man, some listeners even had tears in their eyes. Scrooge's recovered emotions touched the audience.

It's natural to start fuming over what the other person has said or done, but a better alternative is to start pondering how we can put her back in touch with her human emotions. What can we say or do that will make such a difference? We can affirm this person even when she might not deserve the affirmation. While she might be surprised, she will respond with gratitude. Her mind-set will be reversed, and this act of kindness can begin to transform her.

Turn the Negatives into Positives

We all have a tendency to retreat when faced with negativity, but we have the chance to charge forward instead. Before the ax falls, prepare yourself with a mind-set that focuses not on what the other person did but on what Jesus said.

Believe That a Good Heart Still Beats Within

Aim at kindness. Even if it's hard to find, at least a shred of goodness is hiding within difficult people. Believing that we can awaken the better side achieves far more than focusing on the negative. While we are not agreeing to meet their illegitimate needs, we are helping them reach a better place in the world.

Love Is Always More Powerful than Hate

Jesus displayed an amazing capacity to offer affection even when faced with death. Two thousand years later, the only thing we remember about Pontius Pilate is that Jesus stood before him. Had Jesus not offered kindness in exchange for his brutality, Pilate would be no more than dust in our historic memory. Love has endured through the centuries.

Jesus empowered us to love. An encounter with Jesus instills a love beyond what one previously knew. Such love can melt the hardness of the person with borderline personality. Our concern and love have that power.

Reflection

The five reflections in this book can help you gain further insight into how to respond to the BPD person. Hopefully, these reflections will also give you personal insight and help you remain positive.

When we are under fire, mentally stepping back and asking ourselves questions can help us make important emotional adjustments and restore balance. Both the attacker and the attackee can profit from the exercise.

What happens when we step back emotionally during a confrontation?

In his 1969 book I'm OK—You're OK, *Dr. Thomas Harris described how our behavior comes from one of three ego states—the Parent, the Child, and the Adult—that describes how we are functioning at a given moment. Emotionally intense memories from childhood are recorded in the brain much like a tape recorder, and these mind-sets have a way of taking over and controlling our thoughts and reactions. Harris noted that we shift among these three states.*

The Child ego state carries the problems, negative feelings, and emotions from childhood. Screaming fits arise from the Child ego position. Eighty-year-old adults can turn into four-year-old spoiled brats when the Child ego takes over. People with BPD are walking examples of the Child ego.

The Parent ego function reflects what we generally call the conscience. It keeps our hostile or angry impulses under control. However, the Child ego periodically overpowers the Parent ego, and that's when people act out. At the time, these people are unaware of what is happening inside them.

The Adult ego state is the mature, evaluative part that considers and probes reality objectively. When the Adult ego recovers control, we once again keep our spontaneous impulses in check. People with BPD don't know how to allow the Adult ego to restore balance and stability when something upsets them. The trouble begins when they are captured by their childlike feelings. Their old emotional problems return in disguise and ensnare them.

Subsequently, when people with BPD attack, we natu-
rally respond from our Child ego position. After the confron-
tation is over, we might find it difficult to believe that we
could have responded as we did. Harris identified why we act
the way we do. It's "not okay" to make others feel "not okay."

The Power of a Question

Asking ourselves a question disconnects us from the old hostile feelings from the past because it initiates the Adult ego function, which evaluates and analyzes what is going on in the present. During self-questioning, we start backing away from our childish emotions.

A person might be shouting at us, but our emotions shift when we mentally step back and ask ourselves, "Do I need to be defensive just because the other person is offensive? Am I really vulnerable?" The mere act of asking momentarily disconnects us from an emotion.

We should ask ourselves some key questions when a borderline person attacks. For example, "Why am I starting to feel emotional?" or "Is this person's anger appropriate?" or "Am I really a victim here?" Write down such questions. Make them short and simple. Think about them. Review them. They can help release you from inappropriate behavior.

And the Other Person?

The more accurately we can pinpoint the emotional need of the person with BPD, the better our response can be and the more significant the shift in the person's feelings will be. Although it can be difficult, we can help troubled individuals get in touch with the contents of their Child egos, the negative attitudes they have been carrying around for so long. Once they identify what gives them their feelings of being condemned, negated, discounted, hurt, or prejudged, then they can come up with their own questions, such as, "Is this person treating me like my parents once did? Does his opinion really matter that much? Am I actually being discounted, or is it just a difference of opinion?"

When we ask a BPD person a question addressed to her Adult ego state, we are drawing her out of her emotional captivity. Consider questions such as these: "Can we step back and seek some objective authority on the matter? Is it possible to evaluate the problem from another point of view?" Whatever causes the BPD person to think—and not just feel—will be helpful.

Once the person with BPD learns to ask such questions when his emotions start to boil over, he can begin to get a handle on his destructive behavior.

Everyone profits from that shift.

Just a few little questions can make a big difference.

CHAPTER FOUR

Figuring Out Where the Cannons Are

Yes, helping a borderline personality can be difficult. But helping and loving anyone can be a struggle because there are so many ups and downs. Don't be discouraged. You might be doing much better than you think. You're beginning to understand the source of the BPD person's problems. This insight can help you endure. Change might not be easy, but it is possible.

Recently, I had a conversation with John Robinson, a retired military officer who had been in every war since World War II. At his age, he truly understood combat. John had been an artillery man. Because these powerful cannons were fired over the heads of the soldiers, John knew how important it was to aim correctly. Firing 155 mm Copperhead artillery pieces or 227 mm MLRS rockets in conjunction with the global positioning system demanded an accurate report of the enemy's location.

We need the same insight when BPD people bear down on us. We need help figuring out where they hide their big guns!

Take Natalie, For Instance

Natalie could come on with a sparkling personality. Highly intelligent, she could speak on any subject—or at least make you *think* she knew what she was talking about. She had a knack for social maneuvering and could rise to the top of virtually any organization. She was particularly masterful with church groups. Natalie would pick out a struggling YMCA that *she decided* needed her talents and zoom in for the take-over. Generally, she aimed for the person in charge and moved in to become his or her buddy.

One administrator, Tom, felt like he had hit the jackpot when Natalie came on the scene. It was always so hard to find volunteers. But in time, she was telling him how to run the organization, directing the other employees, and bypassing the administration when decisions needed to be made.

Tom became uneasy with what he saw happening around him. Natalie had taken over too large a space in the Y. Beyond being helpful, she was manipulating the entire system. While he hated to use the word *conniving,* he felt like he was caught up in a scheme of some sort.

Members began to complain. People felt that Natalie was manipulative and that she pushed members aside if they didn't agree with her. Tom decided he had to confront Natalie.

One afternoon, Tom met with her and outlined the issues.

Natalie's eyes narrowed. "You're accusing me of being deceitful?"

"N-no," Tom stammered, "I'm trying to make sure we are all on the same page."

"Really?" Natalie raised an eyebrow. "I come here to a Y that's in the ditch with a leader who doesn't know Sunday from sic 'em. I pitch in to pull you out of the hole you've dug for yourself, and now you suggest I'm a calculating schemer?"

"Listen, Natalie. We are grateful for all you've done. You have certainly made a great difference in the lives of our members. I'm only talking about a few irritations that have come to my attention."

Natalie stood up and leaned over his desk. Jabbing her finger in Tom's face, she hissed, "The problem is that you are incompetent. Moreover, you are ungrateful. That's the problem with most organizations today. They are run by jerks with no ability. *You* are the problem!" she shouted and stomped out of the Y.

Because he was so disturbed by what had happened, Tom immediately went to a counselor for assistance. Tom told the counselor the story and asked what he had done wrong.

The counselor smiled. "Did you believe what the woman accused you of doing?"

Tom blinked. "Well ... well, I guess I did."

"That's the problem," the counselor said. "You believed her."

Tom's mouth dropped slightly. "What?"

"You accepted her charges as true. You came away believing you were the problem. She made you think you were the issue. The difficulty wasn't you. *It was her!*"

Natalie had dive-bombed Tom, and as the explosions went off, he assumed he had done something wrong. The *real* problem was that Tom didn't know how to protect himself. He didn't recognize the cannons were being fired until it was too late.[1]

Figuring Out Who Did What to Whom

Borderline people have a talent for firing on unsuspecting people before those people even recognize that a war is going on. Because BPD people come on with such boldness and self-confidence, we tend to assume they might be right. Tom fell for Natalie's line of attack because he's a nice guy who assumes the best about other people. That was the mistake. The problem wasn't him.

BPD people can be so difficult to understand because they are caught between two extremes. On one hand, they appear totally self-confident and can sound grandiose. Anyone who seems so certain must know something we don't—or so it seems. Once we buy into that facade, we're hooked on their line. In truth, their internal world is actually operating at the other extreme. They struggle with worthlessness.

Though we might not observe it, they constantly swing between feeling exceptional and believing they have no value. They present a picture of very high self-esteem while actually having very low self-esteem. Their confrontations and personal exaltations are an attempt to cover up what they are actually feeling and experiencing internally.[2]

Tom felt overpowered, but weakness was at the center of Natalie's personality. However, pointing out the contradiction will get us nowhere. In fact, people with BPD might hit us with the nearest handy object because they feel the secret of their sense of inadequacy must be protected at all cost. They certainly don't want to hear this insight from those they are attacking.

Most folks like Natalie cannot let themselves recognize their own limitations. Their social skills allow them to hide the bottom-line issue not only from everyone else but from themselves. When people like Natalie have adaptive skills and present themselves well, they can hide their fears. However, when they go too far and are cornered, they bring out the cannons. To the surprise of their audience, they explode. That's when the truth becomes evident.

In the past twenty-five years, America has experienced significant social disintegration. The divorce rate has risen higher than 50 percent and has set many children adrift. The number of latch-key children floating through the community has dramatically increased.[3] The bottom line is that many children grow up feeling they have little value. One of the leading causes of death among teenagers is suicide.[4] The feelings of worthlessness create such anxiety and depression that some kids finally take their own lives. BPD people often come out of these situations.

That's the problem confronting the Toms of this world as well as the rest of us!

• •

Don't forget that BPD people have an internal undercurrent of anger.
They might explode for reasons that have nothing to do with the conflict at hand.

• •

What They Can't See

When BPD people fire their cannons in our faces, we tend to assume they know exactly what they are shooting at. Unfortunately, they don't. As a result, they shoot everyone in sight. We must remind ourselves of this as the artillery roars.

In the 1980 film *Ordinary People,* Mary Tyler Moore played a narcissistic mother whose self-absorption ruined the most important relationships in her life. The mother denied the loss of her favorite son in a boating accident and had grown cold toward her other son, who had made a suicide attempt. She was determined to maintain the appearance of perfection and normality in the midst of an abnormal situation. When her surviving son confronted her for the last time, he wondered whether she was capable of truly loving anyone. Rather than dealing with the issues, the mother left the family. The son and father got the tragic emotional bomb blast.

These overpowering, aggressive people are actually struggling with pain and low self-esteem, and their weakness prompts their actions. When the steam stops coming out of their ears and they settle down, usually a cloud descends on them, and they feel depressed and dejected. Because they can't allow themselves to grasp the struggle in their internal world, they are trapped in their own pain. While they make us want to run, the truth is that they are desperate for love and understanding. Our task is to develop the skills to wade through the emotional garbage long enough to finally help them find the acceptance they profoundly need. Sure, it's a hard task, but if we take the New Testament seriously, it is one Jesus left for us to do.

Double-Checking the Unseen Terrain

How can you know if artillery is hidden in the trees? Peter Kuiper, president of Christian Counseling Ministries, developed a narcissism assessment questionnaire that can identify who is likely to shoot at you. His questions are in abbreviated form here, but they can help you develop an accurate sense of what you are dealing with. Can you answer yes to many of these questions regarding the person confronting you?[5]

Entitlement

- Do they expect special treatment?
- Do they thrive on adoration and admiration from others, seeking it out regardless of the cost?
- Do they roll over people without noticing the pain and irritation they cause?
- Do they feel the world owes them glory and respect?
- Do they seek out people who can help them maintain their sense of importance?
- Are they insensitive to how they affect others?
- Do they appear to not care about other people?

Exploitation

- Are they manipulative and controlling?
- Do they maintain a position of influence and power while insisting it's all for the good of the other person?
- Do you detect that they alternate between idealizing themselves and later devaluing themselves?
- Can they jump back and forth between caring and being completely indifferent?
- Do they often resort to put-downs or highly critical judgments?
- Do they sometimes appear to assume they have a right to ignore others?

- Do they rarely admit personal failure and participate in blame shifting?
- Do they seem not to care about how their behavior affects others?
- Do they not hesitate to shame or con others?
- Are they not bothered when they make other people uncomfortable?
- Are their relationships superficial and shallow?
- Do they make you feel off-balance or somewhat "crazy" at times?

Depersonalization

- Do they seem to genuinely lack empathy?
- Do they lack significant feelings for others?
- Do they treat other people like things?
- Are they good at convincing you of their goodness—and of your own badness?
- Do they retreat from genuine human need or ignore others' pain?

Image Keeping

- Do they promote their own self-image?
- Do they use people as an extension of themselves?
- Do they treat disagreement or disobedience as disloyalty?
- Do they see themselves as special or unique?
- Are they deeply bothered when other people diminish their self-image?

Watch for the characteristics in this questionnaire because they will help you recognize that you are not the problem. If you can answers a significant number of these questions in the affirmative, the person likely has BPD.

. . . .

Remember:
You're not the battlefield.

. . . .

What Can Be Done?

After answering the questionnaire, you might have discovered you are dealing with a loved one who has borderline personality disorder. You might be wondering if anything can be accomplished. Is there a cure? In the past, many experts did not believe that BPD responded to treatment, but they have now rejected that idea. We now know that this disorder is treatable. While not everyone recovers, many people do change. Certainly, the symptoms can be reduced.

No one can predict how a person with BPD will respond to treatment, but the option is available. Even with persons who do not totally recover, the reduction of the symptoms is so remarkable that the treatment is recognized as being highly valuable.[6] You can be hopeful.

The tests for BPD are usually scored on a scale running from *possible* to *likely* to *severe*. In other words, this is not a blanket diagnosis; instead, there are degrees of the disorder. Some people may only occasionally act out, whereas others stay in a state of anxiety. The person you are concerned about might have a milder problem than someone else.

The following are some options that have proven successful. You'll have to do more research into each of these therapies on your own because it is beyond the scope of this book to go into detail about them, but this will give you a starting point.

- *Dialectical behavior therapy.* This approach teaches skills that help the client learn how to tolerate distress and how to stabilize emotions. The client is then able to maintain healthier relationships.[7]
- *Schema-focused therapy.* Early life events are often at the root of the problem. This therapy confronts maladaptive ideas the troubled person carries and helps him adjust.
- *Mentalization-based therapy.* In this approach, the therapist helps the client become aware and recognize her mental states as well as what is happening with others. Thoughts, feelings, and wishes are surveyed for insight and understanding.
- *Transference-focused psychotherapy.* This approach to psychotherapy focuses on the relationship between the client and the therapist to investigate and help reduce the symptoms when the person with BPD acts out.
- *Medication.* When used in conjunction with psychotherapy, medications can play an important role in recovery. Some of the most commonly prescribed medications include antidepressants, anxiolytics (antianxiety medications), antipsychotics, and mood stabilizers. And although the results are not yet fully in, researchers are exploring treatments using omega-3 fatty acids.[8]

In some cases, people with BPD will have highly intense emotional experiences that could require an overnight hospital stay. While hospitalization may seem extreme, it can be an important approach in a crisis.

You can rely on professional assistance when BPD issues get out of control. You are not in the struggle alone, so hang in there and know you can tackle these problems.

What's Going On?

Although borderline personalities understand that relationships are important, their perspective of other people is driven by two basic needs: *power* and *control*. They might initially back off after an argument, but to fulfill their most essential needs, they must stay in charge and maintain their "king of the mountain" positions. Once we recognize how power and control operate in their behaviors, we'll have the insight needed to begin to handle their push-and-pull attitudes.

While the manipulative person may have little or no insight into what they are doing, these self-absorbed persons developed their motivations early—somewhere between fifteen and thirty-six months of age. During these developmental years, they received emotional injuries that set the stage for the rest of their lives. Three common parenting practices shaped their need to stay in command. If or when we have children, it is worth remembering what happens when a child is not raised in a constructive, consistently loving manner.[9] Here's what can warp a personality.

1. The Indulged Child

We are all born with self-serving tendencies. Self-preservation demands that our basic human needs be met. We cry when we're hungry and scream when injured. That's just normal and natural behavior. The so-called terrible twos reflect our need to gain control of our lives as we develop physically. Being defiant is not abnormal. We can't help wanting to be in control of our toys: a toddler will jerk a toy away from another child and yell, "Mine!" without giving it a second thought.

Theologians have called this inclination "original sin." Even the first human beings had a proclivity for getting what they wanted rather than accepting what was best for others. As children go from lying on their backs and kicking their feet to crawling around the house, they naturally grab everything in sight as if the objects belong to them.

Psychologists call that development "individuation." Children are breaking away from total dependence on the mother and learning to think for themselves. They are reaching out for everything in the process of becoming a person in their own right. A baby must grow into the awareness that he is a separate, self-directing entity. Problems develop when he does not also learn how to curb these behaviors.

The indulged child expresses these tendencies without restraint. When parents fail to provide discipline, the spoiled child assumes being difficult is the norm. She decides she can be incessantly demanding, and difficult behavior is an everyday occurrence. At age forty, this same person will still act like she is four years old, and you had better get out of her way. The truth is that she lacks internal discipline.[10] She has missed the lessons that restraint teaches.

When a child experiences a parent's disapproval, he starts learning about boundaries. He begins to develop a conscience. His need to act out disruptively is controlled. When discipline comes in a loving atmosphere, the child remembers he has value even when a parent must curb his behavior. As a result, a healthy person emerges with a sense of worth for other people as well.

But here's the problem: when these lessons aren't learned, difficult behavior follows. The child develops a sense of indulgence and truly believes she is above control. A sense of self-worth is turned into self-pandering. She needs to stay in personal control of situations and the people around her.

One man with BPD, Bill, momentarily gave a thought to how his forceful behavior affected his wife, Tracy, and he didn't want to be seen in a negative light (which is also a self-serving tendency). But once that moment passed, he was back to controlling Tracy's behavior. At forty, he was still an indulged child.

⊛　⊛

Discipline is a necessity for a healthy child!

⊛　⊛

2. The Mistreated Child

Abuse has become an epidemic in American society. While the most recent emphasis has been on sexual abuse, small children are often abused physically, mentally, emotionally, and certainly verbally. Some children seem to grow up and avoid carrying the weight of these experiences, but most don't. Instead, they harbor hostility and anger toward the authority figures in their lives. A result is that these damaged people tend to be selfish, defiant, and often aggressive and hostile. Subconsciously, they have a fear that they might not survive.

Prison psychiatrists have discovered that a disproportionate number of inmates were abused as children. The most severely damaged children can turn into psychopaths who exchange their anger for another's pain. Sadly, this problem can go on for generations, handed down from abused children who have now become abusive parents.[11]

While physical abuse is obviously dangerous, many parents fail to recognize how verbal abuse can haunt a child for decades. Name-calling, belittling, criticizing, and never being affirmed leave scars on a child's psyche. When their sense of self-worth is diminished, children struggle with performance. They might feel that nothing they do will ever be good enough and end up being a doormat for the rest of the world.

Tracy's problem was her acceptance of Bill's attacks. Although she wasn't an abused child, she functioned with a self-depreciating attitude. Her problem of feeling unworthy allowed Bill to walk all over her. No one should allow themselves to be demeaned.

- -
The effects of abuse can last a lifetime.
- -

3. Contradictory Parenting

Love is a powerful force that allows children to grow up knowing that they have value. However, when love is fractured or inconsistent, a completely different type of message is etched into their thinking. When babies aren't held often enough, fed on schedule, or changed out of wet or cold clothing, they begin to develop a destructive idea about their parents. Memories of a neglectful parent can affect a child's capacity to care or return affection. Moreover, if the negative situation continues, the child can come to think of herself as a "bad child," which can destroy her self-esteem. These tendencies will produce hostile, narcissistic, and controlling behaviors.

Living in constant chaos, violence, or continuous upheaval produces dysfunctional behavior and distortions in a child's personality. The child can seem shy and quiet but has a hidden capacity to explode and become destructive. As he matures into adulthood, the borderline person develops an undercurrent of hostility simmering in his personality. Associates learn to be careful around him, lest he attack for some minor reason.[12]

People with BPD can switch from loving to despising someone for few apparent reasons. For example, they might show up at work and proclaim how fantastic their boss is. They say they have found the perfect job. No one could be happier—at least for a few weeks. Then one day, they start complaining about how insensitive the employer is or how unfriendly the staff can be. As suddenly as these complaints appeared, they are gone. The "switcheroo" routine leaves everyone trying to figure out what has happened. The truth is, the problem began and developed when these individuals were six months old.[13]

When a sense of being "out of control" starts in infancy, the result will be a highly controlling adult. They feel they must compensate for any possible chaos by keeping everything in predictable order. To do so, they can't trust other people. They can only feel certain everything will turn out all right by keeping every important aspect of their lives tightly controlled.

* *

Remember:
Borderline personalities struggle to trust
anyone!

* *

As a result of their need for control, they usually become black-and-white thinkers with a limited ability to tolerate ambiguity. Their developmental experiences shaped their perspective of people, ideas, and situations as being either all good or all bad. Unfortunately, the world is far grayer. Every day is filled with ambiguities, and they have difficulty knowing how to respond, so they often reject these "gray" situations out of hand.[14]

Another problem arises with parents who want their children to grow up in a certain way regardless of the child's abilities and capacities. To an outsider, these families look like normal people performing in normal ways. But they are not normal. Their parents have projected an image onto them that they are "special." They begin to see themselves in grandiose ways. Whoever they were naturally intended to be is lost as the parents force their own expectations on the children. The children realize they must live up to their parents' ideals if they are to be acceptable. Of course, no children can accomplish these goals, because when they bring home achievements, they discover their parents have just built larger trophy cases. These children are caught in a trap of continued feelings of worthlessness. As a result, they strive after power and control to keep their internal worlds in order.

These three categories are not all-inclusive and do not cover every behavior, but they give us insight into and perspective on why some people can be so difficult to handle. These categories also tell us about the therapy people with BPD need to become balanced and well-adjusted people in a world they can neither control nor dominate.

How Serious Can This Problem Become?

In 1987, *Fatal Attraction* was one of the major motion pictures of the year. It demonstrated how far a seriously flawed borderline personality will go when acting out her psychological problems. Michael Douglas played a New York attorney named Dan Gallagher who got involved with Alex Forrest, played by Glenn Close. After a mutually agreed-upon fling, Dan tried to separate himself from Alex, but she refused to accept the fact that their relationship meant nothing to him. The plot continued to escalate until Alex wielded a butcher knife and attempted to murder Dan and his family. *Really* scary business!

Why don't these people get help? Often they do seek out a counselor, but they tend to move from counselor to counselor when they don't get the answers they want. When the counselor attempts to produce real change, they jump ship. They will begin to hate the next counselor they turn to for similar reasons. The problem is that therapists are in the business of bringing change, and BPD people only want to be placated.

Fortunately, Bill and Tracy's problems were not this serious, but they needed insight to keep the relationship on solid ground because the marriage had already become shaky. Bill desperately needed to explore why he couldn't stop controlling his wife's behavior. Tracy had other relationships that would improve if she became less defensive and more assertive.

Remember:
Insight changes perspective.
Perspective produces insight.

A Few Tips to Help

What can you do when you're trying to see the other side of the mountain? Along with the insights we have gleaned from this chapter, here are a few more ways to prepare yourself.

Practice Disaster Resistance

People in earthquake zones have learned to build resistant structures. They know a serious shake will happen, and they have planned ahead of the event to be ready. Like these folks, you can brace for an emotional shock. Do it now, and you'll be prepared when it's necessary.[15]

Prepare Psychologically

As you read these pages, jot down your insights into the inner workings of people with BPD. Remember how they think and what you can expect. Keep in mind what might have produced their behavior and what this indicates. Rethink your responses so you can aim at more than just a reply when a problem arises. If you are not acquainted with thinking in psychological categories, now would be a good time to start a new way of relating.

Take Pain Precautions

Where does it hurt when you are under attack? Sometimes people feel angry, defensive, hurt, or afraid. Think about exactly how your inner emotions react.

The person with BPD can present a ton of defenses—rage, projection, blame, black-and-white thinking, and so on. Whatever the approach, you can end up feeling like you've been thrown into a trash can. Figure out what pains you the most, and then develop a defense based on your insights. Then, when the blows come, you'll be ready to sidestep the assault.

Living on the other side of the mountain can certainly help.

CHAPTER FIVE

A Second Look at Anger and Boundaries

Anger is a tough issue to handle.

Many highly competent professionals can't manage their own anger issues. A Ph.D. or M.D. degree does not make them immune to anger. Sooner or later, everyone gets tripped up! Because borderline people often major in volatility, we need to give more attention to the problem of anger management.

Consider Paula and Greg

Let me introduce you to Powder Keg Paula. She didn't know people called her that behind her back, but Paula was a walking time bomb. Her husband, Greg, came in for pastoral care because he did not know how to handle her erratic behavior. In addition, Greg struggled with depression. Paula pushed him so hard that he felt it might be easier to end the marriage than try to work through her anger eruptions.

My associate pastor, John, got caught up in the problem when he tried to make arrangements for Paula's father's funeral. She came up with a number of requests that didn't fit a Christian funeral and wouldn't take no for an answer. Because her father had been married twice, she thought singing "Love Is Lovelier the Second Time Around" would fit well next to a soloist singing "How Great Thou Art." After John said no for the third time, Powder Keg Paula went off like a rocket at Cape Canaveral. She screamed into the phone with such a loud, shrill voice that John hung up on her. Nothing new—just pure Paula.

Greg didn't need to explain the situation when he came into the church office. Because of John's experience, I already knew.

Greg first had to work on himself. He couldn't change Paula, but he could adjust his response to her behavior. Whether she improved or not, the problem was an opportunity for him to grow.

Let's pause at this point and consider what this means for you. All of us have to struggle with angry and aggressive people. Most people initially assume that the aggressive person is the one who needs to change. But that approach usually only worsens their behavior. They are already convinced they are right and others are the problem. We can't win on that battlefield. Regardless of *their* intransigent behavior, we can do something about *ourselves*. Greg quickly recognized this fact.

Greg had never been good at self-discipline. He had learned to be passive and to let others make many of the decisions. Paula could really run with that attitude because it allowed her to roll over him. Strangely enough, his nonresistant approach proved to be part of the problem. Greg first had to learn to stand up on his own two feet and recognize when proper limits were being violated. He had to realize that encroachment was a violation that had to be confronted.

Greg's next step was learning that it was acceptable for him to get angry. He was very hostile, but he "stuffed" his feelings so well that no one ever guessed that he boiled inside. Greg had grown up in a home where getting angry wasn't allowed. From his earliest years, he got in trouble if he let himself express any form of irritation or annoyance. As a result, he had become passive while sitting on feelings he needed to express.

Greg had a right to be angry with his wife when she used her wrath to push other people around. She was abusive, and he needed to alter her behavior if possible. What Greg didn't recognize was that his hidden anger always came back as depression. He had to release what was stored from his past to get rid of the dark feelings. We cannot bottle up anger without it becoming destructive to us. Greg needed to learn that anger is a normal reaction when we feel violated.

In time, it became clear that Paula's anger was misplaced emotion. She had been abused as a child, and those harmful experiences built the powder keg inside her. Paula was mad about a past that no longer existed. She kept aiming her guns at people who had nothing to do with why she continued to hurt.

Here was the problem with Paula and Greg's marriage: She had misdirected anger, and he had suppressed hostility. Both parties had to take off their blinders on their past and look honestly at the source of their negative emotions. Both needed help.

Greg's discoveries about himself changed how he dealt with his internalized anger and how he dealt with Paula's anger toward him. At first, Paula remained hostile, but she began to realize her explosions were counterproductive and could destroy her marriage. She didn't want that. After several sessions, Greg's depression subsided, and that signaled real progress. Paula began to seek genuine change.

Paula's problem was harder to solve because she didn't want to confront her childhood abuse to become free of her uncontrollable rage and resentment. With professional help, she allowed these damaged sensitive areas to heal, and a gentler person emerged. Powder Keg Paula became a more appropriate Nice Person Paula.

What Have We Learned?

Looking at a case study such as this provides helpful clues. Greg hadn't learned how to handle his own anger, so he lacked insight on how to respond to Paula's outbursts. He had to recognize that being passive got him nowhere. Does this provide you with any useful ideas?

Paula's problem with misplaced anger caused her irritations to become exaggerated. Both Greg and Paula were being defeated by their misplaced feelings. In Paula's case, she was hurting other people, and that had to stop.

Hopefully, Greg and Paula will be mirrors that will help us see our own reflections more clearly. The following are some lessons we can learn from angry people.

1. They Can Help Us Learn about Ourselves

You might not know what is wrong with angry people. Nevertheless, they offer a highly important opportunity to know yourself better because their anger shakes up everything inside you, and your own unexpected issues bubble to the surface.

The church gives us the ideal for who we are supposed to be. We should follow the teachings and examples of Jesus of Nazareth.

When angry men attacked Jesus, He met them with compassion, and that's what we want to do. Unfortunately, we often walk out of church with good intentions that don't materialize.

Why don't we change? Because those lessons are abstractions, and we must see ourselves in the hard, cold light of reality for change to occur. When someone pounces on you like a tiger, what emotions are aroused? Fear, combativeness, resentment, hate, animosity? That emotion is a clue that something is a motivating undercurrent in your life. You get a peek behind the curtain at how you tick and what must change. Once that feeling bubbles up, grab it and look closely at its meaning. You've got important evidence in your hands.[1]

2. They Can Help Us Bring Our Personal Needs into Sharper Focus

What do you actually want to be like? I remember during a church war how the nicest people turned into gossips, warriors, deceivers, and in some instances, downright liars. However, every last one of them professed to be a follower of Jesus Christ. But their behavior betrayed the truth. Obviously, they didn't want to be like the people they actually were—but they didn't change, and part of the reason was their lack of in-depth perspective.

Too often a tragedy, a death, a personal loss, or some serious problem beyond our control forces us to get serious about who we really are. Reading this book might have such an impact. Running into a person who attacks us emotionally could lead to insight. At such times, we must step back and ask ourselves, "How do I keep myself from becoming that person I don't want to be?" Our needs come into clear focus.

The Christian faith challenges us to exchange hate for love. We can't do this for others, but we can work on the issues within ourselves.

We live in a country where politicians often treat one another like dogs and hate-filled terrorists unleash their wrath on others. Road rage takes lives simply because someone got in somebody else's way. How can we avoid such scenarios? Of course, the answer is love. Angry people help us keep that goal in mind.

3. They Help Us Consider How We Affect Others

Anger is such a self-absorbing experience because agitated people have little sense of how their behavior affects others. Of course, we don't live for the approval of other people, but we do want their respect and appreciation, all of which is lost in a heated encounter.

Stormy exchanges allow us to step back and reflect. They give us pause to consider if there is a better way to relate when a conflict is brewing. Insight can follow, and we can end up in an improved place.

Building Better Fences

Greg had to think long and hard about what he would allow Paula to do to him. How did he want other people to respond? He had to consider his limits and how he would maintain them. He had left the gate wide open in several places, and he didn't want any more soft or spongy boundaries. To achieve his goal, he had to do three important things.

1. Be Willing to Support Your Limits

Because he had always been passive, Greg struggled to stand firm, but he realized that he really could do so. He gained the courage to stand firm by recognizing that his boundaries were meaningless unless he fully supported them. He came to see that it took conviction to stand behind his intentions. He had to recall how his father had frightened him and remember that psychological size is far more intimidating than physical dimensions. Greg recognized that he could resist the fear of the past. These discoveries were a new beginning for him. He would stand behind the limits he had set.[2]

2. Make Your Boundaries Realistic

Boundaries are not self-serving but are limits to ensure respect and cooperation. Greg is not asking Paula to jump through a hoop; he's asking her to stop yelling and being demanding only because she feels irritated. Refusing to be treated in a demeaning and debasing manner is normal and should be acceptable to any thoughtful person.

For example, Greg could say, "Anyone can occasionally feel stressed, but you can't take it out on me by raising your voice and becoming volatile." Such a boundary would be reasonable and good for both Greg and Paula.

Paula, in turn, has a right to tell Greg when he is being passive and avoiding a decision. She could insist that he express his true opinions without her becoming explosive. Allowing the other person to have freedom of expression without reprobation is realistic. Both parties can live with such boundaries.[3]

3. Let Others Know Your Limits

When you start to change, you will need to make sure problem people know your boundaries. You must be clear about where the lines are drawn. The other person must *completely* understand.

Success demands that there be no surprises. You want total clarity. Communication will be smoother when the other person knows you are not accusing him or her of anything. You are simply being honest and forthright.

In his poem "Mending Wall," Robert Frost wrote, "Good fences make good neighbors." He was right on the mark. Good boundaries make for good relationships. This path will keep you on the right track, regardless of who steps across your trail.

Laughing It Off

Nothing defuses anger like a good laugh. You must make sure the joke is not at the expense of the person with BPD, but gentle humor can break the tension and completely change the climate when a fuse is about to be lit.[4]

Humor also conveys good intentions. You are no longer a walking target but a friend. When humor is part of communication, it signals a noncombative style. Another way to do so is to make "I" statements instead of "you" statements. Saying "you" tends to have an accusatory sound, which sets off a BPD person. On the other hand, "I" responses indicate how you feel and do not put the other person on the spot.

When you use humor, the person with BPD hears a friendly ring to what you say rather than an accusatory jab. Everyone can relax.

If humor doesn't help or the joke goes flat, here are four responses you want to avoid. M. L. Heldman calls these "The Four Don'ts." They can help when your attempts have not worked.[5]

1. *Don't defend.* Trying to dig yourself out of a hole through self-defense can make you look foolish or guilty for merely making a mistake.
2. *Don't deny.* Denials tend to make people look childish.
3. *Don't counterattack.* Striking back tends to aggravate and set off BPD.
4. *Don't withdraw.* When all else fails, people tend to run to get out of there before it gets any worse. Remaining passive and silent will hurt you and accomplish nothing with the person with BPD.

Hopefully these "Four Don'ts," as well as the other suggestions, will help you become more effective in your communication with borderline people and defuse the anger bomb.

CHAPTER SIX

Madder Than a Hornet

Anger is a normal part of the human experience and a proper expression when human values are violated. The problems arise when anger is misplaced and inappropriate. Borderline personalities aim anger at the wrong target. The source of their hostility began years before they met us. That's the problem we have to contend with. In *The Verbally Abusive Relationship,* Patricia Evans wrote that an addiction to anger arises from the powerlessness of the abuser. The strength of their heated responses began in their fear of incapacity. Evans's book describes the danger that occurs when anger becomes a daily expression. Eventually, the habit controls the person.

Because anger is an important part of the BPD individual's personality, a deeper examination of the issue is in order. Moreover, when you encounter these persons, you have to learn to deal with your own resentment.

Interestingly enough, BPD people might walk away from a personal explosion feeling relieved because the pressure inside has been released. They probably have no idea that the cause of the eruption was their own pent-up emotions, and nothing is actually settled. The people around them feel bad, but borderline people might feel good because their anger usually gives them a sense of control. Standing back and examining our own anger always has value. As we understand ourselves better, we will have more insight into the attacker.

Salve for the Irritations

Anger is not unusual. It happens to everyone, regardless of his or her psychological makeup. Anger came with the package when we were born. Every person is capable of the entire range of human emotions. The great psychiatrist Karl Menninger didn't believe in the idea of a criminal mind. Rather, he concluded that *everyone* has the capacity for criminal thoughts. Albert Einstein had a similar notion. Both men recognized that we can think up anything without intending to follow through.[1] For example, Ruth Graham was once asked if she had ever considered divorcing Billy Graham. "I've never considered divorce," she said. "Murder, yes, but not divorce."[2] You get the idea. A little salve helps.

The New Testament tells us that Jesus was angry when He drove the money changers out of the temple (Luke 19:45–46). He was furious over the fraud and abuse He observed. While it may surprise some, the Old Testament has much to say about anger. Of the 455 references to anger in the Old Testament, 375 refer to the anger of God.[3] If God gets angry, we shouldn't be surprised when we do. Sounds rather normal!

History doesn't offer much help in understanding anger's role in our lives. In the Victorian era, anger was considered a barbaric intrusion. When things didn't work out right, men could get angry, but the emotion was forbidden for women. It was also believed that men were more rational and women were overly emotional. Men could be trusted with resentment, and women weren't equipped to handle it. Obviously, the Victorian age is gone, and those ideas have gone with it for the most part.[4]

Today, we know there is little difference between how men and women feel emotionally. Anger is universal and not particular to any group or sex. Failure to come to grips with this reality only gives us additional problems. More salve will be needed!

Consider May the Martyr

May appeared to be glued to the wall. When she showed up at church, she could barely express herself and tried to hide behind the doors. May always sat in the back row and hurried away from the church the minute the service was over. In personal conversations, she spoke softly and was hard to hear. The pastor slowly became acquainted with her. In one of his counseling visits in her home, May opened up and told her story. She saw herself as a martyr, and she allowed her first husband's abuse to haunt her long after she left him.

She had traveled halfway across the United States to escape her husband, who beat her when he thought she got out of line. Because of his overbearing influence and poor advice, she had to leave behind her son, whom she longed to see. May happened to move into a house near the church, and that's why she walked in one Sunday morning.

The pastor immediately recognized her deep unexpressed feelings. Only after a few minutes did anger surface when she told her life story. He knew she was living in a highly unhealthy position, but she passively accepted what she considered was her fate.

In the next session, May was reluctant to express her emotions, but the pastor persisted and told her it was normal to be upset by injustice. She certainly appeared to be the victim of manipulation and needed to release her pent-up anxiety.

May finally took a deep breath and described how her son was taken from her. The longer she talked, the more demonstrative May became. At first, tears slipped down her cheeks, and slowly they increased until May screamed about how her controlling husband made her cower for fear of what he might do next. She beat on the arm of the couch and shouted, "I should have killed him!"

Obviously, no one wanted that alternative, but the outburst expressed how deeply she felt her pain. In her childhood, May had learned that anger was displeasing to God. She was afraid to face her own feelings because she thought God would punish her. The pastor helped her see things differently. May was a profoundly angry woman who had never learned that she needed to release these concealed feelings. Once she did, May was on her way to becoming a different person. The people in the church came to know her as a warm, affectionate person. The difference? She had learned to accept her anger and release the idea of being a martyr.

More Insight

In *Good Women Get Angry,* Gary Oliver and H. Norman Wright describe anger as the forbidden emotion.[5] To the surprise of many people, they detail how anger is not a sin but a legitimate and valid emotion. Their insights can help people like May accept their reactions as normal and acceptable. The Bible underscores these insights. Scripture says, "'Be angry and do not sin': do not let the sun go down on your wrath" (Eph. 4:26). In this passage, Paul is actually quoting a Psalm:

> Be angry, and do not sin.
> Meditate within your heart on your bed, and be still. (Ps. 4:4)

In our terms, he was saying, "Get upset, but think it through. Then release your negative feelings!" The scriptures find no value in ignoring what makes us agitated. The Bible's point is that we should not harbor animosity.

Oliver and Wright note that the real issue is how we express what bothers us. Because borderline people are not in touch with the source of their animosity, they express their irritation in exaggerated and misplaced ways. That's where the trouble begins.

Get Acquainted with Your Friend Mr. Anger

Mr. Anger is a friend because he makes us aware of problems on the path. Irritation is an internal warning of trouble ahead. Our interpretations of these problems may not always be entirely on target, but they help tell us what is correct. These appraisals make us aware of what could harm us or what is destructive.

Anger is a divine warning system, like the flashing lights at a train crossing. Because we are born with this capacity, we can truly believe that anger is a God-given response. At the same time, we should be aware that anger is not the same as hate, aggression, loss of control, revenge, and hostility. When fear lingers and grows too fast, the result can become loathing and intense aversion expressed as malice. The helpful emotion has turned into a different creature. The carryover is the same with revenge or lingering hostility. The emotion is no longer a warning light but has turned into a sword.

Hate is the milk of anger gone sour. When a person allows the sun to go down on ill will day after day, the resentment deepens until the emotion becomes revenge. Evil wins the war. One can be angry with someone without the slightest desire to hurt him. On the other hand, hate keeps looking for a point of attack.

May the Martyr came to a turning point when she recognized she could be extremely angry with her ex-husband without desiring to destroy him. She had every reason to be resentful for how he had treated her, but that didn't mean she would go out and buy a gun to shoot him.

We have all been victimized by people who didn't have our best interests at heart. Whether the cause was misinformation or pure hostility, these people wanted to hurt us. They might have even seen themselves as God's tools for vengeance. Of course, we all want satisfaction against such people. But "wanting to attack" is not the same as "attacking." We must deal with the presence of hurt and anger while (as the psalmist told us) not letting the sun set on the negative feelings. Take care of it!

Letting Go

People with BPD can't let go of something they don't know they have. When they make us angry, we can pay attention to what has happened and make the right adjustments. Here are some suggestions that can help you.

Don't Stuff Your Feelings

Anger usually emerges as your heart starts beating faster. Your face might get flushed or your voice might become more shrill. Your body is saying, "The train is coming down the track. Watch out!" But you don't have to internalize these reactions. Whether you go home and hit a punching bag or beat the wall with your fist, you must let the emotion out. If you keep anger inside, it will come back later as depression. Let's stay away from that alternative.

Figure Out What Set You Off

You might want to make some notes or keep your thoughts in a notebook. Think through what happened and come to grips with what affected you. Get a handle on what bothered you the most. You might discover you had every reason to be upset, but you need to think through how you will dissolve the feeling.

During the civil rights era, I was in a restaurant with a person of color and was refused service. The waitress would serve me but not my friend with dark skin. I became so angry that I wanted to throw a glass of water through the front window. After an exchange with the management, we walked out. After considerable reflection, I ended up writing a letter to the editor of the local newspaper. The paper published the letter, and my experience spread across the town. Not long after this story hit the streets, the restaurant changed its policy. My anger had produced a positive action.

Make a firm decision to use your anger constructively. Maybe little can be done about some situations. However, if you can make a decision that brings about a positive response, you will be on your way to making the world a better place. You will turn negative emotion into positive action. After May quit being a martyr, she joined a group that helped other women survive similar problems. She gave advice and provided insight based on her own experience. She helped many people. Turned outward, May's anger became the source of comfort.

You cannot make people with BPD follow a constructive path. They have to make those decisions for themselves, but you can model a better way. When people with BPD receive insight or kindness in response to their misguided assaults, they might see a path they didn't know was there. Your anger might just turn them toward self-discovery.

Reflection

Every now and then, random thoughts run through our minds, and we wonder why we have to keep on dealing with obnoxious people. Haven't we put in enough time trying to work with difficult folks? Why not simply blow them off?

First of all, we can't. When they are family members, social acquaintances, church members, or colleagues, they don't go away. Compassionate people can certainly become exasperated with their antics, but reflection reminds us they won't disappear.

Second, we can grow through these difficult encounters. The struggle with adversity has the capacity to make us stronger. As has been previously suggested, we come to know ourselves better by working with troubling people. They lead us to personal insights. In addition, persistence makes us stronger. Of course, wrestling with their problems is not fun, but it does increase our insights and renew our endurance. In the end, we ultimately discover it is worthwhile not to retreat.

Third, these people need our concern. Everyone struggles to recognize that attackers need help—but they genuinely do. These people have thorns in their souls and need assistance in removing them. The past has infected them with an invisible disease that requires warmth and understanding if the malady is to be healed. And we might be the only ones who can make the difference. Only love and insight can remove those thorns. When we are willing to offer compassion, we have chosen an important and admirable task. We can do the job!

Of course, each person is different, but here are a number of steps we can take that have universal application. Anyone can improve if she chooses to do the following.

Pray about the Problem

Often people wait until they're in a big mess before they pray. Why not reverse the procedure and pray first? When you sense there's a problem at hand, start by asking for divine guidance. Divine insight is the ability to understand in a manner that exceeds your capacity to know. The Holy Spirit often gives such a gift when there is a need at hand. Ask your heavenly Father to guide you.

Consider the Circumstances

While your anger toward the intrusive person might be entirely justified, animosity is still destructive (to you as well as him). Simmer down and allow for a cooling-off period.

Remember that the person with BPD has the problem—not you. Your goal is not to get even but to improve a difficult situation. Keep reminding yourself, "I'm going to be constructive, no matter what he does!"

Reconsider

Ask for divine empowerment to help you see the issues in terms of the other person's needs and point of view. Try to fathom what that person "feels like" when she is being antagonistic. For example, if she was hurt in the past, does she assume you will probably hurt her today? When low self-esteem swallowed her emotions, did she lose the ability to see things rationally? When a person with BPD nails you, being constructive is certainly difficult, but the effort increases your own ability to climb steep slopes. You can do it!

Wait

Give yourself plenty of time to let negative feelings settle. A little time can become a cushion. While you are waiting, ask for guidance in understanding how to approach the situation. Think about what a constructive next step might look like. You want to know how to approach the difficult person in a manner that opens locked doors. Don't be in a hurry. Delay won't hurt anything.

Reflect

Analyze your own feelings that were aroused during a nasty encounter.

Did the experience make you feel small, inadequate, out of control, afraid, or something else? What can you learn about yourself from this situation? Finding out important insights about yourself is extremely valuable. What started out as a bothersome confrontation can turn into an unexpected opportunity for personal growth. Greater understanding of yourself is a reward for your forbearance.

The Difference One Can Make

On one of the docks in San Francisco stands a magnificent statue of Mahatma Gandhi. The great leader who brought liberation to India strongly advocated nonviolence. Having been the victim of slander, abuse, and prejudice, he insisted that kindness was stronger than malice, thoughtfulness more effective than rage, and benevolence better than annoyance. Gandhi not only believed these ideas were true; he practiced them. In the end, India was set free.

If one man could liberate a country by turning the other cheek, perhaps we can set one person free with a similar approach. It's worth the effort.

CHAPTER SEVEN

The Children's Hour

Seldom does anyone consider the stair-step effect of what border-line parents pass on to their children. Generally, these kids grow up assuming that erratic behavior is the norm. Sadly, they conclude that their struggles are the same as every other family's. They don't know such destructive behavior is not normal.

Jane's father and mother lived near an oil field, where her father worked as a "roughneck," moving huge pipes while drilling for oil. The family's church taught that the father's role was to discipline the children *and the wife*. When Jane's mother was fed up with her husband's demands and accusations, she would start throwing dishes, glasses, and anything else that was handy.

The screaming and fighting terrified little Jane and her younger brother, John. John had no idea what was happening, but he stayed frightened every night. Each evening, Jane crept out of her bedroom and watched the brawl before running back to bed and pulling the covers over her head. Jane lived with the fear that one of her parents would kill the other.

Because of gender identification, Jane felt her father's fights with her mother were an attack on her. After the fights were over, her mother would break down and cry. Jane always took this personally and worried about whether her life was also threatened. She was sure her family must be cursed. With nowhere to hide, Jane lived in constant fear.

Fifteen years later, Jane was scared of men. She was awakened by nightmares. Jane was an attractive young woman, but she retreated from relationships with men. Whenever she began to get close to a man, she would warn him about what she would do if he ever hurt her. Usually, the men didn't know what to say.

Jane's depressing memories often erupted during professional counseling. She thought her father wanted to be a good parent, but he never made the grade. Jane had many internal struggles. She recounted a memory from when she was five. Her parents had divorced, but her mother struggled to pay for the children's expenses. Jane started living with her father and the woman he had moved in with. Far from matters improving for Jane, her new stepmother didn't really want children around, since they cut in on her time with Jane's father. Jane didn't believe her world could get any worse. But it did.

Passing the Baton on to the Next Generation

Professionals who work with the children of borderline parents know everyone in the family is affected.[1] Jane's brother, John, was badly confused because he had witnessed his father hurting their mother. While John knew how deplorable his father's behavior was, he would often blurt out the same expressions and become equally insensitive. Jane couldn't understand why John would act this way.

During counseling, Jane discovered that children often identify with the more aggressive parent and can end up being like them. Children are often both drawn to and repelled by the parent's behavior. Their ambivalence leaves them confused about other issues as well. They may end up struggling to figure out where their lives are going.

While Jane's father never physically violated her, he often told her how sexy she looked. His off-color remarks only added to her apprehension. After she went to college, he sent her letters filled with suggestive innuendos. Jane finally gathered up these letters and took them to the counselor for his evaluation.

The therapist explained that the comments were a form of emotional incest. While nothing physical occurred, her father was attempting to make her into a substitute spouse on an emotional and verbal level. Jane began to recognize how destructive this man was to her and her mother.[2]

Approximately one in twenty females end up having sexual intercourse with their fathers or stepfathers. One in fifty males have the same encounter with their mothers or stepmothers. The incidence of emotional incest is much higher. One young divorced mother continued to sleep in the same bed with her son until he was a teenager. Instead of encouraging normal peer relationships, she treated him as an intimate acquaintance. The effects of such behavior can be highly destructive.[3] In Jane's case, her father's actions compounded the effects of what she experienced in childhood. Because she harbored a deep-seated fear of men, without help, Jane was likely to pass her fears on to her own children. She couldn't get over her problem quickly. The memories were burned in her mind.

Borderline persons leave these sort of imprints. Their children don't understand what is going on and end up with scars. We have to remain concerned about these children!

Tattooed with Poison

The effects of borderline people can be permanent, and the experience with them can become like a tattoo etched in the skin that will never go away. With time, these imprints always blur and contaminate the person's thoughts. Because a professional can help remove the stain, the injured need help as soon as possible. This is the prime reason the problem must be addressed.

Our earliest images of God are shaped by the primary authority figures in our lives. Generally, the father in the family fills this role. The dependability or irresponsibility of the parents shapes the way we believe God acts. A harsh, punishing parent tends to produce a God of judgment and retribution. When the parent is the enemy, God the Father will be also have harsh intentions. Many people reject the idea of God because of a destructive experience with a parent.[4] We must be sensitive to this problem for the sake of the child's stability.

As strange as it might seem, when children say their prayers at night, they are actually praying, "Dear heavenly version of my earthly father." Jane desperately needed help to work her way out of this dilemma. Even with her distorted view of God, Jane had gone to church throughout her childhood and even memorized scripture. In Sunday school, she had been taught that God was her friend. Her acquaintances reinforced that position. However, Jane carried an emotionally different perspective. Her memories of her father injuring her mother conveyed the opposite conclusion. God *felt* more like the enemy, and people tend to respond to what they feel far more than what they think.

Parents with BPD often impart confusion to their children. Until a therapist helps them unravel the puzzle, these children consider disorder to be normal. They often conclude that distance from the divine is best. At worst, they shut down the possibility of any communication with God.[5]

Jane's counselor pressed her to compare her heavenly Father with her earthly father. Slowly, she developed a new insight. Her father was not God Almighty. He did not create the heavens and earth. As obvious as this conclusion may be to some, the emotional realization had a dramatic impact on Jane's thinking. She was released from the bondage she had felt for years.

Not long after that discovery sank in, Jane recognized that not all men were like her father. She had to be discriminating and pay attention to what each individual said and did. However, she also learned that she must not read their behavior through the lens of her childhood years. Certainly, some men could be abusive, but she could weed out men with her father's characteristics.

Yesterday's tattoos were being eradicated.

Lessons from Jane

Jane can help us make several significant discoveries. These discoveries can help everyone, but most importantly, they apply to the children of BPD persons. Consider your own situation as you read these insights.

Don't Hide the Facts

No one wants to bare their family secrets. However, not talking about the struggles can be more destructive. If we keep the skeletons in the closet, we end up feeling the responsibility is entirely our own. These hidden stories often grow in the dark. Only a breath of fresh air, the light of day, and the grace of God can clean out the closet.

We must encourage the children of borderline persons to be forthright. A little nudging will help pry open the door that has been kept locked way too long.

Find an Appropriate Friend

We don't want to share our stories with people who won't respect them. A friend is a sensitive person who will appreciate our struggles and keep confidences. When we discover such people, we need to hang on to them: they are hard to find. Their ability to care and listen to us can be more important than anything else. At the same time, professional help is essential. A good therapist often becomes such a friend. Of course, a therapist is already trained to listen constructively and knows how to respond in a helpful way.

Believe a New Day Is Possible

We are often our own worst enemies. We sometimes expect that nothing can improve, and unresolved anger eventually turns into depression. Walking around with a cloud over our heads makes everything appear dark. We must not allow the sky to blacken with no hope for change.

Once we know that our heavenly Father wants only the best for us, we have a reason to look toward a better day. In many places, the Bible celebrates the consistency and goodness of God. We can trust that better days are ahead. Children of BPD people need this insight most of all.

The Borderline Person in the Family Is Not God

Remember that while our early experiences shape our view of God, those thoughts are not final. We must not allow negative memories to obscure a positive present. The mountains we climb will give us a much broader view of what is ahead than what we experienced in the valley. We must see our heavenly Father for who He is *now*—not what we might have thought yesterday.

Jane would be the first to tell us that our relationships at home will affect every other relationship in our lives. We can't hide from our fears or conceal our anxieties. Eventually, they will contaminate us if they are not unearthed. Negative encounters are what they are, but we must examine them, take them apart, and resolve the issues. Then it is time to move on. The children of borderline parents can do so—and so can you.

CHAPTER EIGHT

Problems in the Pew

A long time ago on a distant planet in another galaxy, churches were well-ordered places of worship where everyone followed the rules. Occasionally, some disagreement surfaced, but it was soon settled according to the accepted procedures. Everyone went about his or her own business, and even people who disagreed treated one another respectfully. Unfortunately, that was a *long* time ago. A galactic war has erupted since then. Today, we live in an era called *Church Wars*.

Borderline personality disorder comes with a wide range of symptoms that run from only a few minor characteristics to many extreme and severe behaviors. The *Church Wars* characters I discuss display the range of some of these characteristics. You can prepare yourself for conflict by recognizing the many possibilities. Here's a list of the characters you can find in the average church.

If Princess Leia is not treated like a queen, look out! She's highly judgmental. Then we have Hannah Solo, who does everything her way regardless of what anyone thinks. And also meet Chewie-You-Up, who constantly spreads destructive stories. The worst is Darth Invader: he has no sense of limits and can cause unmitigated chaos in any church. In the end, the church reflects the dark side. Get ready for *Church Wars*.

Does my little parody sound unrealistic? Tour a few churches, and you can meet this cast of characters under many different names. While they may not have the pathology of many BPD persons, they can be just as destructive.

Because churches are voluntary organizations in which members are not hired and are rarely fired, people assume it is open season for any sport they want to pursue. Those options run from shooting blame at the pastor to initiating a corporate-style takeover of the finance committee or other committees. Usually these assaults take place behind the scenes or begin over a cup of coffee at a local café, but they are just as destructive as someone running a car into a telephone pole.

Let's take a second look at our *Church Wars* cast and what they represent. Borderline personalities come with these qualities.

Princess Leia: These types believe they are special. Because they feel they are exceptional, they conclude they can operate by their own rules. Often they are "take-over" artists who push people aside.

Some years ago, I received a telephone call from a woman I had occasionally worked with; I also knew Margie, her sister. Margie considered herself the "queen" of any organization she was in. Her sister had been diagnosed with a fatal illness and knew death was near. Her sister had called me because she was terrified that "the queen" would descend on her while she was dying and take over her lingering life in the hospital. She didn't want her own sister around because Margie's treatment of people could be ruthless.

Hannah Solo: These types don't care about what other people think. They are simply indifferent. They often function with a bulldozer mentality and plow ahead with no regard for how much dust they kick up. They're not interested in taking over, but they want to make certain every decision goes their way. They circumvent the rules, the group, and the usual procedures.

The problem is that they think they know better. They are often intelligent and insightful. The fact that they will be right in a good number of cases makes it even more difficult to deal with them. Regular procedures can roll along fine until they become cavalier. At that point, they brush people aside and consider others irrelevant. Boom! The church has a problem.

I observed a talented church leader functioning with a Hannah Solo style. George had been important in the business world and retired with a significant income. George knew how to run a company. In the beginning, he assisted the pastor in a number of duties. However, as I watched, I began to sense a corporate take-over was in the works. George was a real end-around runner. People began to sense more was going on than met the eye. Before long, the pastor had a problem. He had done nothing wrong, but George's maneuvering had boxed him into a corner!

Chewie-You-Up: You always think old Chewie is your friend—until you overhear him talking *about you*. People once called this type a gossip, but that sounds a little antiquated today. The point is that these types know how to dish out the dirt. They are in the business of conveying grapevine stories, and they love to spread idle tales. Like a vacuum cleaner on two legs, they suck up every story in sight and then regurgitate them when the next person comes along. Spreading rumors is their vocation.

Darth Invader: These types really are from the "dark side" of the force. You don't see them much of the time, but they have a sixth sense about when to show up during decision-making times. The Invader types often don't attend church services regularly, and visitors have no idea who they are. However, Darth and his tribe are quite willing to wait until the right moment comes along to strike. Often they research the rules of the organization so they know exactly the right points to attack. When their moment arrives, they hit with destructive force. They have no conscience about wrecking a church and will follow their objective until the roof caves in.

Let's return to earth and meet a couple similar types. Ellie had a mania for spreading stories. Her ability to dig up innuendos was simply amazing. Because she had a part-time job cleaning houses, Ellie specialized in going through her employers' drawers and then making judgments about what they might be up to. When she found men's clothes in a single woman's front closet, Ellie concluded an affair was going on. She began spreading that story at church. However, the clothes belonged to the woman's brother! Unfortunately, the damage had already been done.

Al Jefferson insisted his passion was for justice. A well-known divorce attorney, he would do anything to win in court. Occasionally, he got in trouble with the Bar Association for his ethics, but that didn't slow him down. At the church, he worked on gathering a group of friends who would do his bidding. Once that group was secure, Al was ready to strike. Two years later, nearly all the church members had dispersed. What did Al do? He moved on to another congregation to start the process all over again.

What Do They Have in Common?

While these types have a wide range of motivations, they all have one similar problem: *they have no regard for boundaries.*

Boundaries tell us where our limits are. They give us the guidelines we should not cross. When these boundaries are observed, positive social relations can be maintained because no one is violated. However, when the lines become blurry or are broken, people get nervous. It's not unlike someone crossing the invisible line that separates your physical distance from other people. When a person gets too close to your face, you start backing away. You sense danger or feel apprehensive.

Boundaries tell us what is appropriate. If someone were to show up for worship on Sunday morning in a bikini swimsuit, that would set off alarms. Such attire is inappropriate for church. Unfortunately, our *Church Wars* friends' dress doesn't tell you what's coming, but their social violations are just as inappropriate as wearing combat boots to a formal wedding. They don't think about what is acceptable.[1]

Each of these types pushes the envelope without regard to other people's responses. If we are going to deal with them successfully, we must look at our own boundaries and examine what we will and will not allow. When we hear destructive stories or plain old gossip, we must respond, "Sorry, I don't go there. I am uncomfortable with such stories." A definite answer stops the rumor train.

One of these gossipmongers began calling people in the church when she heard a prominent leader's family was in trouble. The response she received from one member was, "Hey, that's divorce talk. It leads to nowhere but trouble. Leave me out of such talk."

The gossipmonger was momentarily stunned, and her invasive project was sidetracked. This is just one example of the kind of response we need to develop.

Your best bet is to take a look at your own sense of limits. How do you set boundaries that stop people from being invasive or from using you as a pawn? Often we don't consider how far we are willing to allow others to go and where we will set up our stop signs. It is important to think through these issues to keep ourselves safe. Let's consider four boundary types identified by Nina Brown, Ed.D., a professor at Old Dominion University. Brown's concern is that fuzzy thinking about boundary lines leaves us open to problems. She gives us four categories to consider:[2]

1. *Soft boundaries.* People with soft boundaries are easy victims for pushy people. Because their boundaries are not firm, they tend to blend into and accept other people's boundaries. They have a poor sense of how and when to draw lines that they will not allow anyone to cross. The result is that people walk all over them all the time.

2. *Spongy boundaries.* These folks struggle with uncertainty. They have better-defined limitations than people with soft boundaries, but they remain ambivalent. They lack the certainty in their personal limits that is necessary to prevent people from taking advantage of or manipulating them.

3. *Rigid boundaries.* People who have been abused or mistreated don't want anyone getting close. Their boundaries are cement walls that keep everyone out or at a safe distance. They are highly selective of who they let come close.

They are unlikely to be victimized by the *Church Wars* characters, but they pay a high price by living in psychological isolation. Not much human warmth gets through to them.

4. *Flexible boundaries.* Folks with flexible boundaries are difficult to exploit. They exercise control and are resistant to emotional contagion. Psychological manipulation has little success with them because they make firm decisions about whom they will let in and whom they will keep out. This position is a target we should shoot for.

Yes, it can be difficult to develop these boundaries. We all have subjects that we know we shouldn't talk about—but we do. It takes commitment and persistence to maintain appropriate borders. However, it becomes easier with time, and it will save you from many problems.

When you find yourself swept up in *Church Wars,* stepping back and looking at what you allow or disavow can help you get a grip on the situation. You don't have to be aggressive or difficult to simply say, "Sorry, I don't go there." A brief but firm answer can keep you out of the hot water that someone else is boiling!

Keeping Borderline People in Perspective

Difficult people can drive anyone and everyone over the edge. Churches aren't any different from business offices, homes, or schools—*except* the voluntary nature of a church can be less inhibiting for borderline people. There's no end to the trouble that can come from the institution's lack of restraints. We need to keep several important factors in mind.

Many congregations start Sunday-morning worship with a prayer of confession. With this prayer, we recognize that we have all erred and need God's forgiveness. No one is perfect, and each congregant must admit to having come up short during the previous week—and that includes the borderline folks!

When we say a prayer of confession, we admit that we have not loved God and other people as we should. No matter our convictions or irritations, we have not responded as Christians should. If we take that understanding literally, we can look around the sanctuary and realize that each one of us has exceeded the boundaries that God has set for us. We must forgive all other people for their shortcomings as well. Reminding borderline people of this fact can be sobering to them. It provides a pause that might slow problem people down and cause them to reconsider their actions. This remembrance also helps us see the borderline person in a balanced light.

Problems will always occur in churches and everywhere else. Today, some people see congregational fights as a sign that the church has failed or is a fraud. Wrong! The confrontations are a sign that the church is a human institution with divine aspirations. Don't be offended when people act like people. Sure, some of their responses are troublesome. Certainly, human differences create collisions. Add an emotionally fragile person, and trouble starts brewing. Just don't let yourself become disillusioned.

· ·

In confrontations,
remember to reflect on the dynamics hiding behind the curtain!
Look both backward and forward.

· ·

Throughout this book, we've been digging behind the scenes to gain a broader understanding of why borderline types function as they do. The objective has been to help you gain insight into and a firm grasp on destructive behavior. When people start gossiping and yelling at one another, that's the time to stand back and consider the motivations behind such actions.

Some years ago, I observed a church squabble developing. One of the leaders had decided the pastor was bringing the attendance down. Never mind that attendance had dropped 15 percent across the United States and that this church was well ahead of the curve. This particular lay leader began saying destructive things about the pastor's leadership. People were confounded as to why he had become such an outspoken critic. After the brawl reached a fever pitch, people discovered that the instigator had tried to sell the pastor an investment that the pastor turned down. His rejection had stuck in the man's craw. The real source of the discontent had nothing to do with the church! Only an insightful examination of the man's motives revealed the actual problem.

When people are upset, a discussion group under the guidance of a competent, informed leader can often prove helpful. However, ground rules must be determined at the outset, and group members must agree on the terms of the discussion. The leader must know how to keep probing for the real sources of discontent and then move to make adjustments.[3]

Take a hard look at what scripture says. The Bible shows us how important it is to be prepared for difficult circumstances. Proverbs 9:7–8 tells us,

He who corrects a scoffer gets himself abuse,

   and he who reproves a wicked man incurs injury.

Do not reprove a scoffer, or he will hate you. (RSV)

The author of Proverbs must have discovered that confrontation didn't work well with borderline personalities. He recognized that hitting one of these folks head-on will probably land us in "hard head" city. Harsh words only bring a harsh response. The history of most churches is filled with accounts of when and where this has been true. In contrast, we make progress through kind, gentle words of encouragement. The Bible infers that encouragement is a better strategy.

Let's go back to attorney Al Jefferson. The public knew his claim of having a passion for justice was a facade. In truth, the pressure he exerted was a cover for anger than seethed beneath the surface. People never approached him about the problem because they didn't want to get blasted.

Finally, his wife approached him about the issue. "I was talking with a court reporter," she began. "She was telling me about an attorney that gets so angry that people run from him. Know anyone like that?"

Al blinked several times and stared at her. She said nothing. Finally, he said, "Are you talking about me?"

"Does that sound like you?"

He nodded his head. "Sometimes."

"Many times?"

"Okay, I get the point. Yeah, I do fly off the handle, and I recognize people can get hurt."

"I'm not condemning you," she said. "I want to help you find a better way to work around these issues."

Although Al took some time to fully grasp what they had discussed, he began to realize he had a problem, and his wife had offered him a new path. She had followed scriptural direction, and it worked.

But be prepared for resistance. Some people never give in. No matter how we confront them, they won't back down. When the issue demands attention and resolution, we need a different strategy.

Matthew 18:16–17 records what Jesus suggested doing in such situations. Jesus instructed that two or three witnesses should go with the person when confronting the problem individual. Two or three persons also can help straighten out inaccurate interpretations by later providing a clear description of what was said and how people reacted. They also provide a safety factor.

Is all this maneuvering necessary in a church situation? Absolutely! We all want a constructive outcome.

• •

Remember:

A church has voluntary membership.

Battles can be fierce.

Don't blame the church.

Recognize troubled members.

• •

Boundaries Will Protect You

Boundaries help you take care of yourself. You have personal rights, and one of them is not letting people run over you. You will be protecting yourself when you set up fences that keep trouble-makers from wandering over into your pasture.[4]

We all need emotional limits that allow us to separate our own feelings from those of other people. You will find freedom from the onslaught of an emotional attack by setting limits of what you will accept. You are only respecting yourself by setting emotional boundaries. You must decide that you are going to live a new life-style and be steadfast in that decision.[5]

● ●

Remember:
"Good fences make good neighbors."
—Robert Frost

● ●

CHAPTER NINE

Mess in the Marketplace

Our self-esteem is always on the line wherever we are employed. Jesus told us to count the cost in following him, and one of the places where we often pay a price is at the office.

Let me give you an example.

Larry seemed like a warm, fun-loving guy. When he first came to work for a charity, people found him funny and clever. Because loading dumpsters and heavy trucks in a warehouse is demanding, workers enjoyed Larry's wisecracks. Employees felt he was a breath of fresh air and entertaining. He was soon promoted to a desk job. After two or three weeks, people noticed that Larry's jokes were actually jabs at people. They weren't quite as funny as they sounded at first. With time, other employees realized that Larry was quite argumentative and that his humor was a facade. The bottom line was that Larry was going to be in charge one way or the other. Jokes were only a springboard to his more nefarious purposes.

The higher-ups didn't particularly notice Larry was taking over the office because the work got done. Larry threatened anyone who didn't produce as he thought they should, and he used subtle threats that he might have something to do with firing people (which he didn't). He had an amazing way of undercutting his fellow employees' self-esteem.

Capable workers started looking for the exit door, fearing what might come next. The staff began to experience a rapid turnover. In the beginning, they had thought Larry might be Johnny Carson in disguise. In the end, they were certain he was Adolf Hitler. How could anyone go from the top of the popularity chart to the bottom so fast? He knew how to use people's self-esteem against them to get what he wanted. BPD people have such a talent! We pay a price when we work with them.

Sorry, but people with BPD *will show up* at the office. While such people can be maddening, we need to understand them in order to know how to respond. To regain harmony, we must gain insight into their behavior. Strangely enough, they actually need our kindness.

Where Did That Guy Come From?

Everyone has a personal history. Because people often share confidences at work, the past can eventually come out. Larry certainly had his own story of how he had become such a difficult person. He had grown up in a highly controlling family. A big man who towered over everyone, Larry's father had been a tyrant who dominated everyone in the family. His mother learned early on not to contradict Larry's father. She did what she was told—for a while. But sooner or later, her patience ran out, and explosions followed. His father didn't like being crossed, and when his mother got tired of the abuse, boom! Larry ducked for cover while his parents duked it out.

Somewhere along the way, Larry learned to smile to hide his anxiety and anger. He figured out it was better to appear pleasant at the outset and save his punches for later. To gain control of a chaotic situation, he started using humor to cover his tracks. Later, when he felt more self-confident, Larry released the deep-seated anger hiding behind his jokes. Because his family situation made him feel out of control, Larry needed to find a way to stay on top of every situation. Humor became his tool for attack. It was strange but effective—for a while. Eventually, the approach wore thin, and then Larry again became the victim.

Working It Out at Work

Most employees are on the job because they need to make a living. They don't come to work to be company psychologists. However, when a guy like Larry is sitting in the desk next to you, you need insight into how to deal with such a person. You can't overlook a person with BPD when he's in front of you eight hours a day. Let's analyze this type of employee from the perspective of what needs correcting in order for better adjustment to follow.

Underneath Larry's jokes and abrasive personality was a guy who actually lacked self-confidence. One of the clues we can remember is that the more inferior BPD people feel, the more superior they try to act. Their personal problems have created a self-centered orientation that keeps them from recognizing why other people cry, struggle, worry, and so on. Their inward focus is entirely on themselves. Surprising as it may seem, their pain keeps them from realizing they are hurting others.[1]

Larry's father's heavy-handedness created an inner confusion that remained with Larry. He wanted to love his father, but his father did things that made Larry hate the man. Eventually, Larry's affection for his father got pushed out the back door. He was left with a cynical view of everyone else. Compassion had been tossed aside in favor of pessimism. Even Larry's sense of humor was only a cover.

When this pattern is repeated enough, the results become pathological. One of the scariest villains ever created is the central character in Thomas Harris's novel *The Silence of the Lambs*. The crazy psychiatrist Hannibal Lecter could appear to be sensitive and concerned. He had the ability to listen intently as if he cared. A gourmet cook and Parisian gentleman, Lecter was also a genius. He forgot nothing and made brilliant associations. The problem was that he wanted to eat people (literally). The man's bizarre behavior was somewhat like our friend Larry, just far more extreme.

Hannibal Lecter was so frightening because he totally lacked empathy. People like Larry have a similar but less foreboding problem. When we have to sit next to such people at work, we must remind ourselves that they have been infected by a disease from their past. They irritate us, but they need our compassion.

But how can we offer kindness when they are pushing us against the wall?

Fixing the Fixation

A fixation is a psychological term for a childhood behavior that got "stuck" and keeps us functioning in that same childish manner. For example, a two-year-old child who kept having his cookies taken away by an older sibling never learned to share. Even though he is now a fifty-year-old man, he still can't bring himself to share with others.

A fixation creates an inability to discover new perspectives or adapt to changing circumstances. Borderline people are trapped by their past experiences. Whether people are like diabolical Hannibal Lector or troublesome Larry, they are enslaved by their painful past.

We generally have trouble dealing with these individuals because we listen to what they are saying, *not what they are feeling*. We must attune our sensitivities to pick up on the emotions running behind the confrontations. We must remind ourselves to listen not only to their expressions but also to their emotions.[2] We need to get in touch with our own similar feelings.

Can you remember a time when you felt defeated? Beaten? Remember what those experiences felt like. When you are able to experience the same emotions, you are in a position to identify with the borderline person. That connection is important and helpful. Can you get in touch with your own emotions when you felt empty? If you can get a grip on your own experience and what you yourself felt in the past, the memory will help you understand what is going on with the BPD person.

Here's an example. Some years ago, I got caught up in a church battle in a parish where I was the pastor. While I had actually done nothing wrong, circumstances kept me from giving a full response, and I was dragged to the bottom with many other people. When I saw no way out of this struggle, feelings of helplessness and hopelessness poured in. Today, if I want to get in touch with someone's feelings when the person has been beaten or defeated, I return to that time in my life. I can again remember the pain of not being sure of what to do next or not being understood by people who at one time had been my friends.

Those memories put me in a position to feel with the Larrys of the world when they are creating chaos. While identifying with what the other person is feeling won't solve the problem, it certainly helps me develop the compassion needed to move forward. Here are some more suggestions that can take you on to the next step.

Change the Seasons

When the opportunity occurs for a more intimate conversation, ask the person if she has ever considered the value of closing one chapter in her life and opening a new one. Just as spring follows winter and adolescence comes after childhood, so it is possible to recognize that we need to close the chapter on a past episode in our lives. When someone dies, the grieving eventually reaches a point when we must close that period and move on. This is also possible with the difficult events in our lives. We need to conclude that we must move on and let go of old hurts. We must not let the pain of adolescence define how we act at age forty. Close the old chapter.[3]

Larry needed to recognize that his father was only one example of insensitivity. Actually, the world is filled with multitudes who consistently treat people kindly. He needed to close the chapter on "Starting to Grow Up" and begin a new one on "Achieving Maturity."

Depersonalize

It's hard not to take an insult personally, but we can remind ourselves that the attacker has the problem, not us. We have to keep asking ourselves, "What's bothering that person?" Remember our earlier reflection on the Child ego state? Asking ourselves a silent question moves us on to an Adult ego position that can evaluate the situation without emotion. Personal attacks hook the child in us; depersonalization keeps us on a more adult level.

A shift occurs in attackers when they discover their words do not affect us. They begin to recognize that their approach isn't working, and they will often shift gears, becoming more compatible and even more thoughtful. The workplace can become a more civil environment when the borderline person recognizes fellow workers are not taking him in the manner he had hoped for.[4]

Find Alternatives

Alternative responses can calm the day. When a verbal assault hits, one might say, "Gee, you look tired. Are you worn out?" Notice how such an exchange expresses concern for the person's well-being. Not bad for an opener!

Here's another example: "It seems like something is bothering you. Do you have anything else we ought to talk about?" Offering openness and concern always throws the attacker off target. When you offer the person an option, *make sure she decides* what to do next. The ball is now in her court.

With these responses, the situation at hand has been reversed, and the BPD person is in retreat. Unexpected doors are open, and that invites him to respond with greater honesty.

• •

Remember:

We are trying to fix a fixation.

Seek options, not confrontations.

• •

And What If Nothing Works?

What if the person won't respond to alternatives and kindness? You've done your best and nothing happened. What then?

Jesus told us to "count the cost" (Luke 14:28). Are these struggles worth the price you pay emotionally? If not, then it is time to move on. You won't be the only one in the office struggling with these issues. Eventually, the powers that be will have to recognize what the troublemaker is costing them.

As a believer, your interest is in working in a place where you can serve God. Your desk can be an altar where you worship by how you do your work and care about others. If this is not possible, then maybe you ought to find another job. You certainly have the right to do so.

Your own self-esteem is an important part of the workplace equation. When a person with BPD pushes you too far and shows no interest in changing, you have a right to decide that the time has come to go. For your own well-being, this can be a valid decision. You might want to discuss the issue with a therapist or professional person with trained insight. Or a conversation with a lawyer might be in order. For your own protection, consider keeping a diary of abusive actions and strange behaviors to support your claims if necessary. Because of the extreme reactions of some people with BPD, you will want to take all your personal possessions with you when you leave. Do not prematurely tell the person with BPD that you are leaving.[5] Simply breathe a prayer and shut the door.

CHAPTER TEN

When We Feel Defeated

Sometimes Christian people fall into the trap of giving a spiritual meaning to a psychological problem. They end up finding it difficult to make sense out of what is happening. Sometimes they justify a confrontation by saying something like, "He didn't really mean it" or "She's just not spending enough time in prayer, and it shows." One common explanation is, "He's not spending enough time studying the Bible." Those are nice phrases, but they don't solve the problem when we're dealing with borderline personalities.

The problem is psychological and must be addressed in those terms. Failure to do so will only end up leaving us frustrated. When the unexpected attack comes, we are rocked back on our heels, thinking we've done something wrong. A highly narcissistic personality can fly through a personal encounter like a runaway lawn mower. Debris is scattered everywhere while the mower goes on down the road, destroying everything in its path. We're hurt and left on the ground. For example, take a look at the issues that faced Rikki.

Rikki's Big Problem

Because Rikki was an elementary schoolteacher, she knew what it was like to handle misbehaving children. Most of the time, she had no problem straightening up the children. Her real dilemma was at home. Misbehaving children could be put in the corner, staring at the wall until order was restored. Unfortunately, Rikki couldn't put her husband, Jeff, in a "time-out" when he acted like an irate six-year-old.

Jeff's behavior had always been unpredictable. Their two children, eleven-year-old Susan and nine-year-old Jim, suffered because of their father's unresolved problem. Here's an example of how the issues erupted:

The family was sitting around the supper table, eating and talking in a normal manner. Susan asked her brother, "Pass the green beans."

"You didn't say please," Jim said.

"Don't be a jerk. Pass the beans."

"Children, we don't need a tiff over beans," Rikki said. "Susan, say 'Please,' and Jim, you pass the bowl."

Jim started laughing, and Susan asked if saying "please" meant nothing to him. Dinner went on again like a normal meal.

"Jeff," Rikki said, "did you pick up the clothes at the cleaners?"

Jeff squirmed. "What are you talking about?"

"You know, Jeff. We discussed this morning that you would get the clothes because I had to be at the school all day."

"I don't know what you're saying."

"Well, just this morning, I said to you—"

"What are you trying to do, Rikki? Make me sound like a fool in front of the children?"

Rikki blinked several times. "Well, no. Of course not."

"You do this all the time. You twist my words until I sound like a moron."

"Now, Jeff, you're making a mountain out of a—"

"Really!" Jeff's voice suddenly sounded like he was attempting to break the sound barrier. "I'm tired of you attacking me in front of the kids."

Susan and Jim looked at each other with a knowing, frightened glance. They'd been down this alley before and knew where it was going.

"Jeff, please," Rikki pleaded.

His face twisted into a grimace of pure anger. "You are always nagging me about matters over which I have no control. Here, in front of the children, you are doing it again. The great almighty schoolteacher pressing her innocent, unsuspecting husband into a corner."

The two children looked down at their plates and kept glancing at the door out of the room. They had heard Jeff's screaming and yelling over nothing and wanted to get out of there.

Tears welled up in Rikki's eyes. "I-I'm sorry. I shouldn't have brought it up."

Jeff stabbed the roast beef on his plate like he was slaughtering the animal. No one said anything. A terrible quiet settled over the evening meal. What in the world was going on?

Identifying the Problem

As strange as it might seem, Rikki's innocent question made Jeff feel inadequate. That's where their World War III began.

Jeff had overlooked a request Rikki made. His issue had nothing to do with forgetting to stop at the dry cleaners. When he failed to complete the job, he felt condemned. Jeff couldn't admit to making an error (even though every human makes them). His fur went up like a cornered bear. The children had already learned never to accuse him of even minor mistakes. Jeff just didn't commit errors!

And what was the bottom line? Jeff couldn't tolerate appearing to be inadequate. Even if it meant rewriting history, he would do whatever was necessary to present himself as competent and adequate even when the issue was unimportant. He would almost die trying to prove the issue didn't happen even if everyone knew it did. Rikki was supposed to pick up the clue and say, "Oh, I misunderstood" (even when she knew she hadn't).

To put it another way, Jeff ignored reality. The truth made no difference to him. His obsession was covering the fear that lurked behind every conversation and action. At the core of his being, Jeff dreaded any mistake because it might peel back the cover and reveal who he feared he was.

The inconsistency in their personalities is one reason borderline people can be so difficult to deal with. They make us feel crazy because they deny what we thought was true. We feel like there must be something wrong with us. We have to fight to make sure we *did* remember what was true. The world gets fuzzy.[1]

However, Rikki was also part of the problem. We need to examine her responses to grasp her part in the uproar.

Rikki grew up in the mountains of Bailey, Colorado. Her father spent two decades working as a carpenter, while her mother was a housewife. The family appeared stable and responsible. But most of the community didn't realize that Rikki's father was an alcoholic who periodically went on binges. Usually, these drunken

experiences happened around their property, so other acquaintances weren't aware. However, Rikki knew about them for sure!

Rikki's father became a different person when he was drunk. A
mean streak emerged and he picked on people. He could even end
up in a fight. Rikki's mother usually got the worst end of the problem and was occasionally slapped around. When circumstances
didn't work out right, her father went after Rikki. More than once,
she had gone to school with a bruise around an eye. Rikki grew up
in a home where chaos periodically broke out. Wild, unpredictable
behavior was expected.

Rikki met Jeff in college and was drawn to him because he had
some characteristics of her father, but she didn't recognize that
included destructive behavior. Jeff wasn't a teetotaler, but he didn't
get drunk. Unfortunately, Rikki didn't recognize the characteristics of a "dry drunk." These are persons who don't get inebriated
but display the same destructive behavior and way of thinking.
They tend to conclude that the world revolves around them and
are self-centered to the extreme. These persons have poor impulse
control. They have little regard for the harm they cause others.
They often engage in magical thinking (believing something
is real that isn't even there) and have fanciful expectations and
dreams. Another important characteristic is a judgmental attitude.
They have learned to inflate their own egos by elevating themselves above others through criticism. Surprisingly, these persons
also judge themselves as being less than others and have low self-
esteem. While Rikki's husband huffed and puffed at others, he was
also generating a low opinion of himself. Many "dry drunks" slip
into a pattern of complacency. Their emotions become listless and

dull. Nothing much excites them. As a result, they head in a self-destructive direction.

Jeff had many of these characteristics, even in college. Rikki felt at home because she had grown up with similar behaviors. With time, Jeff became worse, and she could no longer overlook the negative results. Rikki's limited perspective and acceptance of her husband's erratic behavior had developed in her earliest years. When she experienced Jeff's explosive moments, Rikki had already concluded *it was always her fault.* Her thinking had been invaded by this idea that she was responsible when things went wrong. The idea had become a part of her personality. Rikki assumed without reflection that she was responsible. When Jeff yelled, she buckled. Rikki considered doing otherwise to be unchristian and belligerent. Of course, her children didn't have this history and immediately recognized something was seriously wrong.

Hiding the Problem

One of the underlying issues was that Rikki had spiritualized the problem. When they met in college, Jeff attended a campus gathering held by Campus Crusade for Christ. Rikki also attended the Bible study and believed Jeff was the man she was seeking. She idealized their relationship and thought it had a divine intention behind it, so she discounted the tensions. While her Christian concern was on target, the way in which she spiritually coated their relationship kept her from objectively recognizing that problems were coming down the road.

Although Rikki held Christian ideals, like so many Americans, she was biblically illiterate. She followed Christian principals in general but had little insight into applying them to her life. She was hopeful but not well grounded. One of the weaknesses in her thinking was the idea that a Christian wife should be completely obedient to her husband (with a heavy emphasis on *completely*). When Jeff shouted, she cowered. That was another example of spiritualizing the relationship.

The arrival of children brought a new dimension to their confrontations. Rikki was forced to recognize that the children had a distinctively different take on their father's reaction. She had to become less passive. However, when she pushed back, Jeff became even more obstinate. Rather than seeking understanding, he screamed louder. The problem was that he wasn't as concerned about being right as he was about staying in control. Jeff demanded that his role as king not be challenged. Rikki had finally grown tired of Jeff always being a control freak. The problem was out in the open. War was declared!

When we seek change, we must recognize how borderline people are likely to function. Regardless of the issue, they intend to stay in the driver's seat. They manage the checkbook, hold on to the credit cards, validate expenditures, and keep their hands firmly on the steering wheel. When they have this bent in their behavior, they will not change easily. You can bet on it.

The time had come for Rikki to seek change.

Seeking the Higher Ground

If you are in a similar situation, you will want to note what Rikki did. She recognized she needed help and sought out a competent professional counselor. Many people call themselves Christian counselors or imply they can help. Check their credentials. Did they attend reputable universities or colleges? Did they study professionally in the area of psychotherapy or counseling? Was their program certified by a state accrediting agency? The exception may be a denominational pastor who studied pastoral care in seminary. The point is to make sure that you're not dealing with someone who shoots from the hip. That can double your trouble!

Rikki found a qualified counselor who knew how to ask the right questions. She recognized that only one or two visits would not correct her problem. In each session, the counselor kept pressing her to consider if Jeff's responses were realistic. What did he ask that was unreasonable? At first, Rikki had a hard time identifying exaggerated behavior. Her thinking had become ingrained with the idea that Jeff must be right.

Finally, the counselor hit pay dirt. "Is there one area where you know he is out of line?"

"Well, yes," Rikki said. "He and I constantly battle over money because he accuses me of being a 'spendthrift.' Jeff says I am unrealistic, but the truth is that Jeff overspends the budget. I never do, and he knows it." Her voice became more intense and her passivity vanished. "He thinks because he receives a salary, he can buy a new car any time he pleases. Buy an expensive suit when he wants! I swear he has no control over his spending. Buys anything that he likes."

The counselor leaned over his desk. "So Jeff has demands that are completely out of line?"

Rikki took a deep breath. "Y-yes. I guess he does."

"There's more?" the counselor asked.

"Well … Jeff is never happy with the sexual side of our marriage. While he complains about limitations, I read the national averages. We are far beyond what is considered normal in America. He is flat-out wrong in his complaints."

"And you accept everything else that he says as true?"

She paused for a moment. "Well, Jeff thinks I drive too slow and am overly cautious when I drive."

"Are you?"

"Frankly, no. I am a defensive driver who tries to anticipate what other drivers might do. Consequently, I've never had a wreck. *No!* Jeff is wrong."

"And with the children?" the counselor asked.

"I don't think Jeff is sensitive to our children's needs. He attacks me in front of them."

"So you've allowed him to run over you at all these points?"

Rikki took a deep breath. "You're telling me that I am far too accepting, aren't you?"

"I'm just asking a question. Are you?"

Rikki got the point and began to rethink her acceptance of what was clearly not true. She had reached a turning point in her life. "What is *really* going on in our marriage?" she asked.

"Jeff wants to stay in control."

Rikki began to nod her head.

Saying Good-Bye to Spiritualizing

To get her life back on a stable foundation, Rikki learned to make three important decisions. When Jeff began to bear down on her, Rikki asked herself several questions that created a distance from the confrontation and helped her rise above the struggle. She would mentally step back and ask herself about what was behind their confrontations. Here are three questions for you to consider.

1. What Is the Bottom Line of the Argument?

Even when the substance of the disagreement is important, it is still essential to remember what is churning in the borderline person's mind.[2] Jeff is not unique in his drive to stay in control. Who's going to have the last word is a familiar theme. Generally, control is the fundamental concern.

Rikki had to consider her responses in this light. To keep herself from succumbing, she had to remember Jeff's emotional need to be in control. One of the exercises that proved helpful was to sit down after a disagreement and write out what they had said. As best as Rikki could remember, she would write out the dialogue as it had happened. Then Rikki began to analyze how the conversation had unfolded. Slowly but surely, she began to recognize the dynamic that went on between them. The better she understood their banter, the more capable she became in responding.

2. Am I Starting to Feel Inadequate?

BPD persons seem to have a knack for cornering other people in an argument and making them feel incapable. Rikki's problem was that she had grown up believing this was always the case, and that attitude had to change. When the feeling of insufficiency began to emerge, she needed to recognize the tendency and refuse to accept what she tended to discount. With time, the pattern began to change and diminish.

Is this difficult to do? Sure. Changing an ingrained perspective is not an easy task. However, learning how to adjust a destructive attitude is essential. You might need to write down your personal issues on a note card that you refer to many times throughout the day. Placing a note on a mirror or the dashboard of your car can provide practical help.

When the other person realizes you are responding differently, he will have to make his own adjustments. None of us can force insight, but a shift in your behavior will certainly help the other person begin to see the light.

3. Where Are the Sensitive Areas?

We all have subjects that leave us feeling uncomfortable. If people call us degrading names, we will respond with hostility. Borderline people are the same—except far more so.[3] The better we become at identifying their "hot buttons," the fewer conflicts we will face.

Because power and control are key areas for clashes and collisions, we must avoid battles in these areas. Often we can defuse the issue simply by reminding the other person that the problem has nothing to do with who is in charge or who is making the final decision. No one wants to be diminished, but weakness is a key area of vulnerability for borderline persons. We might need to remind them that we can disagree without implying anything about their capacities.

If you have made a transcript of one of your disagreements, you might look for where you punched one of those troublesome buttons. Identifying what starts the war is critical. Ask yourself questions like these: What is she worried about? Where does she think loss of control will lead? Is she obsessed about making the right impression? Does she fear what might happen if she loses control? Is she worried about the possibility of being blindsided? The possibilities go on and on, and you need to identify the hot zones.

Don't be discouraged if it takes time to figure out the puzzle going on in the BPD person's adverse responses. Once you've identified the minefields, you won't get caught in unexpected explosions.

. . . .

Remember to ask yourself:
What is the bottom line of the argument?
Am I starting to feel inadequate?
Where are the sensitive areas?

. . . .

Reflection

Saul and David are two of the most interesting characters in the Old Testament. Their relationship is a study unto itself. Saul was basically a country boy during the period when Israel was a nation of independent tribes. When he showed up to fight for Israel, Saul was head and shoulders taller than anyone else and quickly proved to be a powerful warrior. Known as a devout Jewish believer, no one doubted that Saul loved God. He quickly became king.

We don't have any information in the Bible about how Saul evolved from being a simple villager to developing a murderous mentality. We can guess that the roots of what would become a serious problem were there from early childhood.

*Stuck in a battle with the Philistines while the giant
Goliath antagonized Israel, a young David showed up and
soon became a hero and close friend of Saul's son Jonathan.
A faithful follower and supporter of King Saul, David unex-
pectedly became the object of Saul's suspicions. King Saul
began to imagine that David would try to steal his kingdom.
We watch Saul evolve into a hateful, treacherous enemy with
every intention of killing David.*

*The encounters when David eluded Saul and the never-
ending chase provide some of the most interesting reading in
the scripture. To say that Saul turned into a BPD person is
an understatement. Do these stories give us any insight into
dealing with borderline people? Interestingly enough, they do.
How David handled himself through adverse circumstances
offers us helpful and important insights. Notice what he did.*

Keep Your Perspective Clear

*Because of his own purity of heart, David remained loyal
to the king because he knew that was the right thing to do.
When the personal attacks came, David knew he was not the
issue. Supporting the Lord's anointed regardless kept him on
tract. The time spent alone on a mountain slope during his
years as a sheep herder had done something important for his
character. He had a strong sense of right and wrong. There's a
lesson for us in his enduring awareness of values. David's clear
ethical sense of right and wrong lifted him above the fray.*

*The stories of David's struggle to stay away from Saul's attacks
were motivated by the divine imperatives that stood behind the*

office of the king. No matter what happened, David would not attack the king. He demonstrated that when people place their ethical values at the top of their list of priorities, they are guided through the struggles by principles, not personalities.

Such an insight can help us stand above the mess created by precarious people.

Remember that you are not a psychiatrist!

The suggestions throughout these pages are meant to help you understand difficult people. Hopefully, these ideas have given you new avenues to walk down when dealing with these people, but remember that you can't change them.

One of the important principles that Alcoholics Anonymous has given us is that change doesn't occur until the person makes a personal decision *to alter his own behavior. The issue is entirely with him. Until he recognizes that his behavior is counterproductive, he stays the same.*

It's said the definition of insanity is repeating the same actions over and over again while expecting different results. Sanity returns when the pain becomes so great that the process stops. Sooner or later, BPD people will come to some form of realization that they are doing something wrong. Then change can follow.

We have to maintain a competent response to their behavior that will eventually turn on a light in their heads. That's not a small task.

Maintain Your Insight—Regardless

One of the important lessons in David's response to Saul is that he stayed with the appropriate behavior regardless of Saul's attacks. His consistency provided the direction that was necessary to avoid going to war with the king. David had an inner sense of right and wrong that he didn't violate. He could be counted on to do the right thing.

Keeping a steady focus is not easy, but it is highly productive. The story of Mahatma Gandhi also provides a picture of how powerful an unwavering focus can be. Time and again, the British believed Gandhi would buckle under their superior military strength. However, they did not understand that Gandhi's commitment to nonviolence actually contained a moral power that would prove superior. No matter what the English did, Gandhi did not change his course. In the end, Gandhi won.

How Can You Accomplish Your Goals?

We must turn our insight into discipline. People often make important discoveries only to forget them a week later. When they remember what their intentions had been, they feel disappointed, but change has still not kicked in. They need a practical approach to staying on top of their decisions. Here's a suggestion.

Write down your discoveries or insights on a small index card. Put the card in your pocket or purse—someplace where you will see it often. Make the sentences short and to the point in a way that will cause you to remember the larger context. Review and study your perceptions at a specific time each day. Keep reviewing these principles until they are etched into your mind.

You could do something similar with this book. Put a paper clip on the pages where you've underlined material that you know is important. Put the book in a place where you will see it at night or first thing in the morning. Go back and keep reviewing.

You won't be sorry.

CHAPTER ELEVEN

Staying on Course

We have already delved into what creates a borderline personality. The loss of authority figures or the loss of the influence of an essential person in a child's young life leaves a vacuum that becomes filled with anger. Only much later in adolescence or adulthood does he allow the explosion to be fully released. Because they live behind an emotional front, BPD people generally guard against exposing their real feelings. They must create and maintain the right appearance. The fundamental goal of every borderline personality is to keep the right persona in place.[1]

Like politicians in an election year, it's not easy for them to keep the right mask on. Qualities like integrity and personal dignity don't count in this game. What's important is self-promotion and maintaining the facade. Because those with BPD carry an inner emptiness, they lack a true sense of themselves. Rather than functioning according to "who I am," they react on the basis of "who I need to be." They have an internal need to preserve that false face. They often operate with a deceptiveness that they hide even from themselves. With time, this phony front becomes confusing to people who know them. People begin to sense they must be wary of such persons.

A spin-off of this borderline disposition is a lack of empathy. This does not mean they do not have feelings and might be insensitive. They can have a genuine concern for the well-being of those they consider true friends. However, anyone outside that circle might find the person to be quite different. A lack of empathy expresses itself in harsh, unfeeling ways. The tendency is to treat people like objects rather than persons. When anyone's emotions are shut down, other people just don't count. Recognizing these possibilities will help us keep the BPD person's attacks in perspective.[2] The following is an example.

Allen the Ax

Allen was a denominational Baptist executive who seemed to be a happy, friendly sort. He greeted people warmly and appeared to care about the pastors under him. Always cracking jokes, Allen seemed quite accepting of everyone. Only after a period did his associates recognize that he was actually highly judgmental and conservative in a way that squeezed out anyone who disagreed with him. He actually had limited theological knowledge, but that didn't keep him from having dogmatic opinions that he expected everyone to agree with. Behind the smiles, Allen was a BPD person with an ax.

"George," Allen said to one of his fellow executives, "I was reading that essay you wrote for a religious magazine. Interesting."

"Oh," George said, "hope you liked it."

"Well, I read it several times trying to make sense out of your position on the Jews. You seem highly accepting of them."

"Of course," George replied. "Jesus was a Jew."

"Yes, yes." Allen waved his hand in a dismissive manner. "But you seem to indicate that they had some favored position with God."

"Sure." George shrugged. "God made a pact with them at Sinai that was renewed with the prophets. Surely you are aware of biblical history. You did study Old Testament history?"

Allen's eyes narrowed. He seemed unsure of what to say, but he didn't look happy. He knew little about the Old Testament. George went back to work, unsure of what had bothered Allen. George knew his position certainly fit any mainstream group of which he was aware. Not so with Allen. The denominational executive realized he wouldn't win any theological debates with George, but that only fired up his resentment. Before his animosity was satisfied, he'd make George pay!

Allen began talking with the clergy, suggesting George had become heretical. "After all," he snarled, "embracing the Jews puts us in a bad light with the people who really count."

At first, the clergy blew off Allen's remarks as nonsense, but that only incited him. Allen got more serious about his attacks on George. He became Allen the Ax and even enlisted the help of some of his underlings to demean George. Finally, the clergy began to suspect Allen was possibly anti-Semitic. Of course, he vehemently denied the suggestion.

Was he truly anti-Semitic? Hard to say ... but that wasn't the root of the problem. He feared George would appear superior, and that was the issue that set him off. Allen was more concerned with appearance than anything else. The problem that boiled within him was not a theological difference in perspective: it was that he might appear less capable than another person.

The people who had to work with Allen the Ax were thrown off course. They not only didn't expect such a tirade; they had a difficult time staying balanced. Allen threw everyone off-balance with what was actually only his problem. George and others later discussed how to react to situations like the one Allen created. How do you respond when you sense something is wrong with the person, not the issue she is pushing?

Uncovering the Cover

As we have already observed, standing back and carefully assessing the situation keeps us from getting sucked into the battle. We gain an emotional distance that helps create stability. In a situation like that with Allen the Ax, additional emotional space becomes vital. We can ask ourselves several helpful questions.

1. What's the Persona They Want Me to Buy?

We all have personalities—characteristics we want the world to believe are really part of us. We grow up with a sense of limitations that we believe can be overcome if we are able to project this ideal on the screen in other people's minds. People want to be seen as movie stars, geniuses, athletes, rich, and so on. In Allen the Ax's case, he wanted to appear to be a great theologian. It's okay to have these ideals until we start believing they are *really* true. That's where the trouble starts because the image keeps us from becoming our true selves. Some people spend a lifetime being someone they are not. In the case of BPD persons, their personal needs keep them stuck in a ditch they have dug.[3]

We need to take a step back and analyze not only what we are seeing but also what we are *feeling*. What does this person on the attack want me *to sense* about her? Does she want me to think she's in charge? That she's important? Maybe that she can be overpowering? Sometimes people want us to think that they are bright or beautiful. Is that what's happening? At other times, they want us to be afraid and to retreat. On and on the possibilities go.[4]

Once we get an idea of what is vital to the person, we will have an important clue about how to respond. By speaking to the image, we can often defuse the bomb. George might have said something like, "Allen, in your position, I'm sure you see the importance of these issues." Or, "Allen, of course someone in your position can be significant in such a discussion. However, I'd like to make a suggestion."

Get the idea? When you calm BPD people's fears, you quiet the tigers hiding in their personalities. The key in a conversation is to go with what you sense is true. Your intuition may offer you the best insight at that given moment.

2. Can I Identify What Values the Person Is Willing to Jettison?

Would discarding a relationship be worth keeping an image in place? To most of us, it wouldn't; to a BPD person, it would. Is winning a disagreement more important than losing a friendship? Again, it is to a borderline personality.

Allen the Ax is not unique. The world of theology is about the pursuit of truth and reality as it grows out of love. And yet today we have forty thousand different denominations because people got angry and walked out. In the name of what was holy and godly, they threw their former friends under the bus. It happens all the time.

In today's corporate and political worlds, relationships are considered marginal. Achieving a higher personal status is what counts. You can see how borderline people can emerge near the top in a business world where winning is everything. Of course, I am caricaturizing the situation to some extent, but you can see how the problem works.

One significant way to deal with borderline personalities is to sneak up on their blind sides. By appealing to their best instincts, you might be able to illicit a more positive response. For example, if maintaining relationships is not important to them, looking good certainly is. Zero in on how they can appear best to the largest number of people.

George might have said, "Allen, as you know (which he didn't), Christians around the world are reassessing their relationship with the Jewish community. We could take a major step forward if we did the same. You might take leadership in this effort."

Is this manipulation? Since the goal is to achieve the best possible relationships and the greatest good possible, I would not call it manipulation. Rather, the action is a form of diplomacy. Our goal is to be adroit and competent in our relationships. Working this out with borderline personalities is demanding, but it's well worth the effort.

Recovering a sense of the values that affect them can be a major help in working with BPD people. Moreover, the effort helps us maintain balance.

3. How Do I Stay Balanced?

Although we should not suggest that they are lying, we must be cautious about taking borderline persons at their word. We need to stay aware that they are aiming at a destination that is not on our map. We must find an elevated place to stand that allows us to have a transcendent grasp of what is going on. An emotionally raised stance allows us to comprehend more than what is being said. Again, asking ourselves key questions while the BPD person is talking will provide the essential disconnect. We might consider whether the person is making sense or whether we recognize a distortion. People with BPD aren't apt to realize that what they are saying is a distortion, or at least, they aren't likely to admit it to themselves. They might sound quite earnest, with a sincerity in their voices that would convince the average bystander. At the point of the argument or confrontation, they might really believe what they are saying is definitely true. Because of this tendency, they can be dangerous and extremely destructive.[5]

A local pastor's wife had this problem. She had become disenchanted with her husband and was attracted to a man in the church. The pastor had no idea this was occurring, but he knew his wife had undergone an emotional shift. The wife began confiding in her close friends that her husband was unfaithful. She would sob and tell her story with passion. You can see where this is going. The wife quickly gained more credibility than the husband. The passionate tone in her voice was convincing. In the end, the church became highly unbalanced.

When such a whirlwind is blowing through, we must remind ourselves to step back and stay out of the emotion spinning around us. To stay balanced, we cannot get swept up in the passion. Objectivity might not be easy to maintain, but we must seek emotional distance.

Going Forward

In the foregoing situations, the BPD persons might have exhibited a great deal of emotion, but we must remember that they attack without empathy. They might have strong feelings, but they are not feeling *with* other people. Often friends might say, "Oh, they are just blowing off steam." True, but steam can burn, and those with BPD won't feel the pain. We must stay aware of this deficit in their personalities. We can sometimes recognize the problem when people with BPD switch completely from one state of hostility to an entirely different passive mood almost in minutes. Our task is to recognize these problems and fly above them so that we can stay balanced.

Because the person with BPD can become vindictive, you need to remember to protect yourself. When you see a distortion campaign coming, think carefully about how you might be a target. If you sense hostility is blowing your way, protect yourself emotionally, financially, and legally. Look carefully at your vulnerable areas and consider where you might be attacked. When the hurricane blows in, put together a plan that can help you.[6]

Probably no one in all of literature was more narcissistic and difficult than old Ebenezer Scrooge. Unmoved by the financial needs of his clerk, Bob Cratchit, and Bob's crippled child, Tiny Tim, Scrooge concentrated only on his own wealth. Scrooge's nephew stayed balanced and wouldn't be pulled into the spiderweb that Scrooge spun at Christmastime. In his three troubling dreams, Scrooge was confronted with the destructive emotions that had turned him into a nasty miser. The story makes a good case study.

A Christmas Carol gives us an excellent example of how we can help borderline people. And such an attempt can help us stay balanced.

● ●

People with BPD have an inner vacuum.
We can try to fill the void with love.

● ●

Reflection

Attempting to put borderline people in touch with their highest emotions is one of the ways we can stay balanced when under attack. Earlier I described these attempts as diplomacy. Maybe you are wondering if they are also biblical. Let's look at the account of Jesus's effect on Zacchaeus.

Although a Jew, Zacchaeus was an agent of Rome, collecting taxes for the oppressors. Undoubtedly, this position made him despised. In Luke 19, we are told he was small in stature. These two factors undoubtedly pushed him toward the characteristics of a borderline personality. The "little man" was defensive and aggressive and didn't get along with virtually anyone—until Jesus came to town.

Because of the widespread reputation of the tax collectors, Jesus probably knew about Zacchaeus well before he came to Jericho. Notice the first thing Jesus said to this conniving thief of poor people's limited incomes: Jesus said He was coming to his house for supper. Rather than attacking and accusing the tax collector, He honored him. Look at the steps Jesus took in dealing with Zacchaeus.

1. Appeal to the Other Person's Best Motives

Jesus's decision to go to Zacchaeus's house suggested to the public that He had a special relationship with the tax collector. Jesus built on his initial contact, adding another layer of positive acceptance. Luke 19 does not tell us the whole story, but it implies something happened during the meal that prompted Zacchaeus to proclaim he would give back what he had taken from people. The tax collector was moved to compassion. Jesus immediately applauded what Zacchaeus had done and proclaimed, "Today salvation has come to this house" (RSV).

2. Build on What Is Positive

When Jesus told the tax collector that He wanted to come to his house, He implied that Zacchaeus would need to change how he dealt with people. Zacchaeus already knew Jesus's reputation because he climbed up in a tree to see Him walk by. He knew what Jesus stood for and that dining with Him meant a confrontation with a set of values he didn't have. Zacchaeus made up his mind to get serious about what this meant for him. Somewhere between climbing down from the tree and the end of the evening meal, Zacchaeus allowed himself to look into his soul and visit secrets from his past. He opened a closed door.

3. Believe in the Person's Self-Worth

Difficult people leave us with an urge to dispense with them. We want them out of our lives, which tells them they have no value. Certainly, Zacchaeus must have experienced such rejection daily as he exacted taxes from the people.

Jesus conveyed the opposite. By coming to his house and eating a meal with him, Jesus demonstrated that the tax collector had value. That evening must have been an exhilarating experience for Zacchaeus.

During that evening, he invited the love of Jesus to become a part of everything that transpired in his life. We are not given a picture of the turning point, but it is implied in the story. The tax collector knew what changes were necessary. Jesus didn't tell him what to do. Zacchaeus recognized the problem. Greed turned into guilt.

While we can't change a borderline person, the love of Christ can. Love does what coercion cannot accomplish. Imbedded in the psyche of a borderline person is a loss that has become part of her reality. To change this deficiency, another reality must enter and fill the vacuum. An encounter with the living Christ accomplishes this need. When Zacchaeus sat across the table from Jesus and looked into His eyes, he saw far more than he could have expected. Possibly, Zacchaeus saw what he could be rather than what he was. Change was on the way.

We have no record of what caused Zacchaeus to be a difficult man who fundamentally betrayed his own people. He probably harbored destructive anger. Behind that anger was probably fear. When people have been abandoned in some way, they carry a deep-seated fear about their own survival. Years must go by before they can begin to reflect on their anxiety. However, the love that Zacchaeus experienced in Jesus pushed that fear aside. The tax collector was liberated from himself.

Very few people live with love at the center of their lives. A wide range of motivations—such as apprehension, doubt, condemnation, inadequacy, or incapacity—lurk behind our thoughts, actions, and hopes for the future. We see ourselves with limitations, not possibilities. When Zacchaeus encountered the love he found in Jesus, that core of his personality was touched. Instead of self-promotion, he burst forth with new generosity.

Can this happen with borderline people that you have to deal with? Certainly.

Many people read the Bible and believe all the right things but have never seen themselves through the eyes of Jesus. When they do, a surprise always follows. They discover truths about themselves that they have missed. As this happened to Zacchaeus, it needs to happen to the BPD people in your life.

But remember, you cannot do this for them. They have to make the discovery for themselves, and the new direction begins by inviting Jesus in for fellowship. While there are many perspectives on what it means "to invite Jesus in," fundamentally we are talking about opening ourselves emotionally to the possibilities and promises of love as the Gospels describe the life and ministry of Jesus. We open ourselves to an encounter with love as the source of our motivations and intentions. We ask for a relationship with our Creator, our Father God, to guide and direct our path for the rest of our days. Because God is love (1 John 4:16), our lives are motivated by this new center that empowers us to be loving people.

What happened to Zacchaeus can happen to every borderline person you meet—and yes, the discovery can be yours as well.

CHAPTER TWELVE

A Friend Indeed!

The old adage "A friend in need is a friend indeed" certainly applies when confronting the chaos created by borderline personalities. Their attacks leave us feeling isolated and alone. Because the assaults may come out of the blue, we are often left mystified and need reassurance. A genuine, confidential companion can certainly be an asset!

Let's go back to the denominational executive, Allen, who had a problem of undermining the pastors who worked with him. Allen's devious attempts to attack people with whom he disagreed didn't stop at the office. His borderline problem spilled over at home as well. The matter finally came to a head when his wife, Alice, decided she could no longer tolerate his behavior. The civil war was about to begin.

Borderline people feel particularly threatened when challenged. Because their difficult behavior generally arises out of emotions they've lost touch with, a question about their capacities can feel like a threat. Underneath the surface of Allen's bravado was an insecurity about his own ideas and convictions. He hid much of this problem even from himself, which made his tirades and angry responses even more shrill.[1]

Alice had lived with the problem for too long before she finally went for help. She found a closed support group (open only to regularly attending members) who listened with sympathy and concern. Alice had always been afraid of confrontations, but the group encouraged her to recognize there would be no change until she was ready to face Allen's explosive responses. Almost holding her breath, Alice went home prepared to oppose Allen's next assault.

Sure enough, it didn't take long for Allen to become abrasive. This time, Alice held her ground. Of course, Allen upped the ante. The screaming got louder and louder, but Alice didn't back down. When she refused to budge, Allen eventually stormed out of the house and slammed the front door. Alice stood there shaking, but at least she had remained firm.

The next day, Allen came in and apologized for his part in the argument. He seemed somewhat mystified about how everything had turned out, but he was regretful. Finally, he hugged his wife. Allen suggested they could go back to normal, forgive each other, *and forget it.*

Alice froze. She had heard Allen use that phrase many times: *forget it.* Those were code words that meant "Don't talk about it again," and that implied "Don't bring up the subject ever." Nothing had changed.

When Alice brought the problem to her support group, they immediately reinforced her conclusions. If any change was to occur, she couldn't let the issue go. Allen had to enter into a process of modification. She couldn't back down. That evening, Alice gave him an ultimatum. Either he would go with her for help and counseling or she would no longer tolerate their home situation.

As was predictable, Allen exploded and dogmatically said no. Alice then told him she was packing and would leave that evening.

Allen was shocked and speechless. Alice marched upstairs and grabbed a suitcase. At that point, Allen crumbled.

When their defenses are broken, their undersides are exposed, and weakness often surfaces. Although they probably haven't recognized it, their explosive behaviors have always masked a hidden inadequacy. However, when that hidden reserve of need is revealed, something good has happened. While borderline people consider this absolute defeat, it is the beginning of the resolution of a problem that has haunted them for years. An important inner door has been opened. Recognizing their weaknesses, they can begin to become genuinely strong.

What caused this shift to occur for Allen? Alice's support group stood behind her. Through her friends, she found the capacity to stand up for what she knew was right. Friends during her time of need provided the encouragement!

Building a Safety Room

I have a home in Oklahoma where the tornados annually come sweeping down the plains. Many people in this vicinity have a special room with concrete walls in the center of the house where they can run when a twister blows through town. This "safety room" provides the shelter needed until the storm blows over. Friends are a similar escape shelter when we don't feel equal to the task of standing up to the human tornado coming our way.

Let's note some of the reasons friends can be so valuable.

Alice found a support group made up of people who had faced difficulties like those she encountered with Allen.[2] She discovered nothing was wrong *with her* when her husband's behavior became too difficult to handle. Other women had lived with identical issues. Their responses helped Alice clear her mind. She was able to fly above his tirades and have a larger picture of the problem.

Everyone needs emotional support. No matter whether the crisis is large or small, having a strong shoulder to lean on helps us stand tall. While we may initially be uncomfortable sharing our struggles, the opportunity to join hands with others adds the props and strength we all need from time to time. A cord of six strands is always stronger than one.

Moreover, everyone can be helped by having a person or group that will allow them to test their perceptions. When the BPD person is someone close and dear to us, confrontations tend to cause us to doubt ourselves. Sooner or later, we question our perspective. An outside objective source can help us nail down reality.

In the beginning, Alice tended to assume she was wrong about the struggles with her husband. She knew he was extreme, but she thought maybe she was off track as well. The support group guided her into a new viewpoint that brought constructive change. Of course, there is a vast difference between a gossip session or people who basically want to control other people's lives and a support group. Generally, a support group gathers around a shared experience of a problem so members can share their journey. A common purpose keeps the group on a constructive and guided path.

Good examples are the Alcoholics Anonymous (AA) or Narcotics Anonymous (NA) groups. Because addiction is so powerful, support group members with the same problem offer sustaining strength. These two groups have the same starting point: people must admit they are powerless over their addictions and want to turn their addictions over to a higher power or to God. Persons in need will have a personal sponsor who is available to them 24/7. By turning to the sponsor, they have new support.[3]

Is admitting that one is powerless over the assaults of a borderline person actually humiliating? At first, the admission might feel humbling, but it is not only honest; it is also the beginning of climbing a mountain we cannot climb alone. Alice's realization that she could not change Allen's angry behavior was her first necessary step beyond the problem. Very similar to AA and NA, the Al-Anon program is for the family members of people with substance abuse. Because most of these persons have developed codependent relationships, they need assistance in understanding how they can work out the entanglements that codependence creates. Support groups can provide vital insights.

And here's another important service that friends provide. Sooner or later, emotional struggles overwhelm us all. Friends who will cry with us allow us to vent our frustration and hurt feelings. Men are helped by someone who will be emotionally close to them. Emotional release is usually necessary at some point.

A safety room can save our lives when a tornado hits. Friends provide the same security when an emotional whirlwind flies through.

• •

Remember:
We all need friends.
They can help sustain us.

• •

CHAPTER THIRTEEN

Forgiveness? Really?

Forgiveness is a cleansing experience.

While releasing the pain that people have inflicted upon us is always challenging, the release is liberating. When a person or group has deeply injured us, we want revenge. We imagine that seeing them humiliated would leave a sweet taste in our mouths. It doesn't.

We are not meant to carry animosity and ill will. Unfortunately, when borderline people unload on us, our natural tendency is to carry the burden for days, weeks, maybe forever. We must learn how to release these assaults so we don't carry the load.

When Hate Ruled the Day

Consider these two experiences.

The German people lost World War I. The armistice proved to be humiliating and put Germany in a difficult position. Depression followed, and the value of the German currency disappeared. The scene was set for the rise of a dictator. Enter Adolf Hitler.

The Third Reich became a slaughterhouse, killing six million Jews as well as a large number of gypsies and homosexuals. By the time their rule ended, anger, animosity, and hate abounded.

I knew two of the refugees from this time of horror.

Hela's family lived in Leipzig, Germany. As the animosity toward Jews increased, her family decided to smuggle her out of the country in one of the Kindertransport trains (a special train to rescue Jewish children). Hela ended up in a kibbutz in what was then Palestine. Life was difficult. Swamps surrounded the farm, and Arabs often shot at the workers in the field. But Hela endured.

Years later, Hela returned to Leipzig and found their old synagogue. When she found the *shamah,* the caretaker, he took her down to the basement, where the old membership files were kept. Written on her family's card was the confirmation that the rest of the family perished in Auschwitz. For the rest of her life, she carried the burden of anger and depression, and she doubted the existence of God. She was not free from the past because she couldn't forgive.

Christians often think that forgiveness is easy—but it is not. When your entire family, community, and locale are wiped out for no other reason than hate, the resentment and personal loss stick. You can speak the words of forgiveness, but the brokenness and the stain of the atrocity leave an indelible scar on your soul. I have no words of condemnation for Hela's struggle. I merely report her experience. Hela and I talked many times about the reality of a heavenly Father, but she couldn't believe in Him because of the pain still lodged in her soul.

I first met Corrie when I lived in California. She lived just upstairs from me in Fullerton. She had settled there after a lifetime spent traveling across Europe and America. Shortly after Hela escaped Germany, Corrie and her family were caught hiding Jews in their home in Haarlem, Holland. Corrie and her sister, Betsie, were shipped to the Ravensbrück concentration camp, where they faced terrible persecution from the Nazis. Her elderly father died in another Nazi camp. After beatings and near starvation, Betsie died in the camp. As the war was ending, Corrie was released in the dead of winter because of a mistake.

Eventually, she recovered her health and began sharing her faith across Europe. When Corrie was speaking in Munich, she recognized a man in the congregation as one of the SS officers who had inflicted severe pain on her and Betsie in the Ravensbrück camp. Corrie recoiled but continued to speak of how the death of Jesus Christ had brought forgiveness of sin.

After the service, the former SS officer came forward and thanked Corrie for the message, which had profoundly touched him. He asked for her forgiveness and extended his hand. Would she shake hands with a person who had inflicted such pain on her and Betsie? How could she? And yet she had just preached forgiveness.

Almost mechanically, her hand slowly came up. Corrie wasn't even sure how she did so, but the love of Christ had worked in her regardless of the dark stain of the past. She forgave the man. After the service, she realized the pain of her terrible experience was truly over. The past was settled. She had undergone a cleansing experience.

Hela and Corrie both had ample justification for hate and abiding animosity. No one who has not gone through their experience can fully grasp the pain they carried. Who can sit in judgment of how either woman handled her struggles? However, the difference that forgiveness made is clear. Corrie found a release from the past and the freedom to go on, leaving resentment, estrangement, and loathing behind. She was free because she had forgiven the man who injured her.

Breaking the Bonds of the Past

The Nazis and their supporters provide us with many examples of borderline personalities. Their confrontations and assaults are always difficult to accept. While our irritations might seem minor compared to those of Hela and Corrie, nevertheless they create deep-seated resentment and a desire for revenge. The only answer for restoration is forgiveness.

Let's explore what forgiveness means.

1. Forgiveness Is Not Negating Right and Wrong

Often people fear that if they forgive, they will be changing ethical rules. Moreover, they worry that they might have to reconstruct the past to make what occurred acceptable.

We must always remember what happened in the past because that is one of the major ways that we grow. Memory is essential. We certainly don't want to erase the destructiveness that someone has caused, because we learn from these past injuries. To forgive is not to condone the sins of the past. When people lied, cheated, manipulated, and so on, they did something wrong. That does not change.

Forgiveness means we look the past squarely in the face and remember the facts as we experienced them. However, we decide we will no longer hold on to the ill will that past actions caused us. Instead, we release our feelings attached to the event. Probably, we will have to make a number of attempts before the feelings are settled.

2. Forgiveness Is Honest

If we are to have a genuine release, we can't allow any phony baloney. We must examine how we truly feel. Often people think that if they have certain types of feelings, then they must have evil residing in them. Nope. That's not reality. When we're happy, we're happy. If we're angry, that's the way it is. Feelings are only feelings.

Forgiveness means accepting the way it was in order to get on to the way it can be.

3. Forgiveness Is Not Weakness

One popular movie image is the rough, tough hero who would rather die than bend. This James Bond 007 personality gets revenge no matter what it takes because he is the strongest of the strong. Some people conclude that to forgive would be ineffective, weak, and a retreat. But the opposite is true.

Letting go of the effects of a misdeed takes courage and strength. When we have been devalued and violated and still are able to stand back and release the problem, we exhibit extraordinary courage. When we pardon other people for what they have done, we show considerable fortitude.

4. Forgiving Is Not Forgetting

Many times, we might truly want to forget. We would like to erase a devastating experience that continues to haunt us. But our minds retain these bad memories, even when they need to store them in backroom compartments. A number of years ago, I was the first clergy on the scene of the terrorist attack on the Murrah Building in Oklahoma City. I stood behind the bombed building as the firemen brought out the bodies, and I prayed for the victims. It took months for me to come to terms with the horror of what I witnessed and still remember. Nevertheless, in order to remember my grandchildren, many joyous Christmases, and a thousand happy times, I must also remember that awful day.

When we forgive, we release the lingering effects of how people have harmed and hurt us. However, these encounters of pain do not disappear. Rather, they find new places in our memories, where they are no more than pieces of the past. We can remember, but we go on to other things and other days.

We must retain the memories of the past to receive the important lessons and insights they offer.

Holding on to What Counts

In the midst of difficult memories, forgiveness means hanging on to what counts. The experiences that hurt occupy only a short space in the past. Because of the headaches and heartaches, those events seem to crowd everything else out. The truth is that once the negative emotions are deflated, they are reduced to no more than another memory.

Borderline personalities are haunted by the original emotions hiding under stacks of memories they have trouble accessing. They end up being controlled by what they can't see.[1] That's why professional help is so important.

At the same time, borderline people can also learn to forgive. They can discover that even what annoys and tends to set them off can be controlled. Rather than store up resentments, they must learn not to let the sun go down on what made them angry. Like cleaning out the bag on a vacuum cleaner, they can empty out the past grievances before they go on to the next day. Cognitive therapy can help people discipline themselves to think differently than their emotions dictate.[2] As much as anyone, people with BPD need to learn to forgive. And they can!

We must remember that the process of being cleansed by forgiveness can take a significant amount of time. One prayer for forgiveness usually won't finish the task. We might have to repeat that prayer many times. The pain of the original incident must subside enough for us to even consider releasing the past. The greater the intensity of the pain, the longer it is likely to take. We don't need to feel defensive about returning again and again to the struggle. Eventually, the power of forgiveness will break through and set us free. Simply keep after it.

Working through past injuries can restore self-esteem. When we overcome the wounds from an assault, we have a new reason for a more positive view of ourselves. Unfortunately, many people cater to ill will from the past. Their souls shrivel while they allow anger to consume them. On the other hand, when we shut the door on even justifiable animosity, we increase our capacity to conqueror these feelings. We deserve applause for such successes.

When we take this step, we are fulfilling one of Jesus's commandments: "You have heard that it was said, 'You shall love your neighbor and hate your enemy.' But I say to you, love your enemies, bless those who curse you, do good to those who hate you, and pray for those who spitefully use you and persecute you, that you may be sons of your Father in heaven; for He makes His sun rise on the evil and on the good, and sends rain on the just and the unjust" (Matt. 5:43–45).

This passage paints a picture of how our Creator deals with all creation. To emulate God's divine actions is a challenge, but it certainly leaves us with new self-worth. The important cue is the instruction to start praying for people who wish us animosity. When we pray for them, it is difficult for us to despise them. We must pray for the grace to forgive as fervently as we pray for our own need for forgiveness.

Steps to Recovery

1. Consider Who Started the Fight

Carefully reexamine the dynamic that popped up when the conversation became heated. Well-intentioned people naturally feel that they caused the problem. People with BPD particularly zero in on people who take their responsibilities seriously. Possibly, the guilt you felt was not appropriate in the first place. Shake off such undeserved guilt.

2. Don't Practice Denial

Forgiveness demands that we face the problem head on. Unfortunately, many people want to rewrite history and act as if the past incident never happened. They want to rewrite the script of past confrontations and minimize their role in the difficulty. Sorry, but there's no forgiveness at the end of that road.

Denial can take strange forms. Take Velma, for instance. Her husband died suddenly from a massive heart attack. Everyone rushed to surround Velma with love and support. The funeral proved to be inspirational, and Velma maintained her faith that her husband was in heaven. However, in the following days, her attitude started to change. She was irritable and would suddenly become angry over nothing. When the pastor confronted Velma about her animosity, she denied having any problem.

As the months rolled by, Velma continued to have emotional explosions. What was going on? She was *mad at God—and her husband*! Velma had been left alone, and she was furious. But she would not admit it. She needed to forgive God (even though that sounds strange) and her husband (as if he had control over dying). Because Velma couldn't face why she was angry, she couldn't free herself.

The pastor could do nothing. Velma was a victim of denial, and any discussion of reality would have only made the matter worse. Denial can be dangerous in a number of ways.

People can also decide to become victims, even when they are not. In Charles Dickens's *Great Expectations*, Miss Havisham was abandoned just before her wedding. Denying all other realities, she became bitter and shriveled because of her anger. As the years passed, she continued to wear her rotting wedding dress. The poison in this woman's life contaminated those around her. She couldn't forgive or forget.

We must be completely honest with ourselves if we are to achieve forgiveness.

3. Seek Wholeness

Desire the best for yourself. You are only diminished by resentment. Rage destroys. You must turn aside and pursue a better, more fully integrated personality. Of course, such a quest demands spiritual growth. To be complete, you must seek the face of God, and that demands an attempt to see the BPD person through the eyes of the Creator. No matter what you feel, your heavenly Father continues to love difficult people, so you must try as well.

As I have said many times throughout these pages, we can't change borderline people, but we can change how we respond, and that can affect them. We also help them when we aim for our own personal completion and wholeness regardless of their actions. Developing the ability to forgive no matter what the other party does is a positive step for our well-being.

4. Practice Forgiveness

Start and end each day by forgiving everyone and anyone you have struggled with. If you make this a daily practice, you will position yourself for maturity and freedom. Breaking the binds and bonds of old injuries is vital for your growth.

Your response remains paramount. Holding back and refraining from blasting someone puts you in a much better position to be helpful in the future. Moreover, your restraint and constructive actions will help you dispel any resentment you might feel.

Borderline personalities can also follow these steps. The source of their problems is different, but making a determined effort to love is restorative. Learning to care about people they once perceived to be their enemies can do important things for them.

• •

Remember:

Forgiveness is cleansing.

• •

A Final Reflection

From page one, the goal has been to help gain a realistic understanding of the borderline personality. By now, you have insight into how difficult borderline people can be. The preceding chapters have offered help in finding a successful way of responding and adapting to their unrealistic demands and harsh confrontations. Hopefully, each chapter has given you significant insights. You might have found new tools for slowing the beast down.

And I hope you've found increased inspiration. You can be an ambassador of light to a person in darkness. The issue is larger than simply making adjustments and enduring. The apostle Paul wrote, "Blessed be the God and Father of our Lord Jesus Christ, the Father of mercies and God of all comfort, who comforts us in all our affliction so that we may be able to comfort those who are in any affliction with the comfort with which we ourselves are comforted by God" (2 Cor. 1:3–4 NASB). Paul wrote to encourage believers to play a role in bringing solace and comfort to people in trouble. Certainly, people with BPD are afflicted. Beyond maintaining a constructive distance, you might be able to provide genuine change. To pursue that possibility, consider the following guidelines.

Don't Be Afraid of the Struggle

Remember that throughout the ministry of Jesus, He faced misunderstanding, hardship, and rejection. Even in His hometown synagogue, the local folks wanted to throw Him over the cliff. Both Sadducees and Pharisees opposed Him when He healed brokenness on the Sabbath. Two thousand years later, we are different because He didn't stop helping desperate people.

One of my favorite insights from C. S. Lewis is that suffering is God's megaphone.[3] The heavenly Father whispers to us at various times, but He shouts when we wrestle with adversity. If we truly want to help borderline people find their way out of entrapments from the past, we must go through difficult experiences. But we will grow through these moments, and God will be right behind us.

We can talk about our struggles with unemotional objectivity *after* the time has passed. But during the controversy, the encounter feels terrible and our views are subjective. When we are plowing through the mud, we might not realize that God is with us as never before. At those times, He is guiding us in our struggle with difficult people.

Again and again, Christians return to the account of the garden of Gethsemane, where Jesus prayed about facing His own painful death. They listen to hear His voice as he cried out, "My Father, if it is possible, let this cup pass from Me; yet not as I will, but as

You will" (Matt. 26:39 NASB). They are reminded of how difficult important decisions are, but following the will of God is infinitely more important.

The Gethsemane prayer encourages us to continue seeking to bring insight and release to people who struggle with their tangled emotions. We never know how much relief and strength we can individually impart to others. Remember that our heavenly Father wants people with BPD to be set free.

Some years ago, a person struggling with severe depression kept acting out in ways that got him thrown back into a mental hospital. When his wife died, his world crumbled. For months, he holed up in an apartment that came to look and smell like a garbage pit. I kept working with him and encouraging him to walk through the darkness. On one occasion, we sat in my office while the man repeated again and again that he was going to kill himself. Each time, I responded that the man would live and be well. Months passed while the spiritual battle continued. Today, the man is not only out of the hospital; he has a job in a local grocery store. The struggle paid off.

People Are Meant to Be Redeemed

While the pathway to wholeness is hard for people with BPD, the goal is so important that the walk is essential. However, many BPD people don't understand that improvement and change are possible. We must challenge them to recognize that they are walking through a dark tunnel and light is at the other end.

You could be an important factor in their coming to see new promise.

Often transformation occurs during the most difficult of times. One of the important figures in medieval times was Ignatius of Loyola, who founded the Jesuit order and developed the *Spiritual Exercises* that changed millions of lives. Ignatius had been a soldier of some significance when a cannonball mangled his leg, and it eventually had to be amputated. In an age with no anesthetics, his many operations were extremely painful. However, as he lay in bed recovering, he discovered a desire to be a servant of Christ and lead others into this new way of life. Pain was his gain. And the world profited.[4]

The transformation of St. Francis of Assisi happened centuries earlier, but his was another story of painful struggle that changed a roaming man of the streets into one of the most significant Christians in history. His redemption also resulted in the first clergy coming to the New World with the Spanish. He prayed to live a life in which injury, doubt, and ill will were transformed into forgiveness, faith, and courage. Centuries later, the change is still occurring.

I could write volumes about the stories of troubled people who later became agents of reconciliation. Their difficult times became the matrix for recovery of a new personality. Change is not easy with people who think about retaliation and retribution all the time. Getting back at those who have offended them is a recurrent theme with so many BPD people. They do not realize how deeply they are locked into revenge. Breaking this cycle is not easy. Often their healing doesn't start until some tragic or catastrophic circumstance occurs.

Nevertheless, should you choose to take on the responsibility, you might be the person who can be there to help when the roof falls in. If you develop a conviction about the promise for change and redemption, you can be an agent of hope.

We Are Not Alone

Of the suggestions made so far, this is the most important of all. As I have noted in several chapters, people with BPD have a special ability to zero in on us with such precision that we feel like we're alone in the world. But the Holy Spirit is with us. We can ask God to guide and lead us through this time and experience. We don't face the problem alone.

In these contemporary times, the philosophy of existentialism expresses the loneliness and isolation that many people feel. The population explosion causes some people to conclude they are only a meaningless dot on the map. With more than 50 percent of marriages ending in divorce, loneliness grows. A high percentage of today's children grow up in homes where there is no father. The accumulation of these factors causes desolation to become the norm.

At such moments, we must remember that Matthew concluded his gospel with Jesus saying, "I am with you always, even to the end of the age" (Matt. 28:20). In John's gospel, Jesus said, "These things I have spoken to you, that in Me you may have peace. In the world you will have tribulation; but be of good cheer, I have overcome the world" (John 16:33).

During trying times, we need to recall these promises and recognize that they apply to us. We are not victims in a struggle going on in the streets or in a face-to-face confrontation with a BPD person. Standing behind us is the Lord of the universe, who will be there to help us work through the struggle.

Love Is the Answer

John was the only apostle who was not martyred. As an old man, he was often carried into a gathering of Christians. As he went among the people, John said over and over again, "Children, love one another. Love one another."

In John's first letter, he wrote, "Beloved, if God so loved us, we also ought to love one another. ... [I]f we love one another, God abides in us and his love is perfected in us" (1 John 4:11–12 ESV). The love John wrote about has the capacity to heal borderline people. In the beginning and the end, we must rely on this love.

So many people have in some way been deprived of the love they need. As a result, they grow up with profound spiritual deficits in their lives. The thought never occurs to them that love might be the healing force in their personalities—but it is!

Stacy discovered this was true just after she had a baby. Having grown up in a highly judgmental church, she had been taught that the nature of God was harsh. She had come to believe in a God who was always watching her with an intention to punish her. Of course, this had a direct effect on her emotional life.

Immediately after Stacy had her baby daughter, the nurse brought the baby in and placed her in Stacy's arms. Stacy was overwhelmed with love for this wonderful gift and held the baby close. Abruptly a divine whisper said, "Stacy, now you know how I love you."

God had spoken, and her understanding of Him dramatically changed. The reverse of what she had been taught was true. She had discovered that God is love.

People with BPD can make the same discovery.

Acknowledgments

I am grateful for the help and insights given by many people in this book who wished to remain anonymous. Their witness has made a difference to many. I particularly thank Dr. Larry Kalb, Tate Wise, and Ramona Hanson for their insights and suggestions. As always, I am grateful to have an agent like Greg Johnson, whose help is so valuable and appreciated.

Notes

Chapter Two

1   Paul T. Mason and Randi Kreger, *Stop Walking on Eggshells: Taking Your Life Back When Someone You Care about Has Borderline Personality Disorder* (Oakland, CA: New Harbinger, 2010), 14.

2   Anthony W. Bateman and Roy Krawitz, *Borderline Personality Disorder: An Evidence-Based Guide for Generalist Mental Health Professionals* (Oxford: Oxford University Press, 2013), 1.

3   Mason and Kreger, *Stop Walking,* 200–201.

4   American Psychiatric Association, "Practice Guideline for the Treatment of Patients with Borderline Personality Disorder," *American Journal of Psychiatry* 158, no. 10 (Suppl.; October 2001): 1–52.

Chapter Three

1   Robert O. Friedel, *Borderline Personality Disorder Demystified: An Essential Guide for Understanding and Living with BPD* (Philadelphia: Da Capo, 2004), especially ch. 12.

2   Friedel, *Borderline Personality Disorder,* ch. 12.

3   Paul Meier and Robert L. Wise, *Crazy Makers: Getting Along with the Difficult People in Your Life* (Nashville: Thomas Nelson, 2003), 63–69.

4   Meier and Wise, *Crazy Makers,* 120.

Chapter Four

1   Lynn Melville, *Breaking Free from Boomerang Love: Getting Unhooked from Borderline Personality Disorder Relationships* (Santa Maria, CA: Melville Publications, 2009), 31.

2   Anthony W. Bateman and Roy Krawitz, *Borderline Personality Disorder: An Evidence-Based Guide for Generalist Mental Health Professionals* (Oxford: Oxford University Press, 2013), 11–12.

3   Robert Firestone and Joyce Catlett, *Fear of Intimacy* (Washington, DC: American Psychological Association, 1999), 5.

4   Arialdi M. Miniño, "Mortality among Teenagers Aged 12–19 Years: United States, 1999–2006," *NCHS Data Brief* 37 (May 2010): 1, accessed May 2, 2017, https://www.cdc .gov/nchs/data/databriefs/db37.pdf.

5   Peter Kuiper, "Home," CrossRoads Counseling of the Rockies, accessed August 27, 2016, http://www.crossroads counseling.net/.

6   J. F. Clarkin, K. N. Levy, M. F. Lenzenweger, and O. F. Kernberg, "Evaluating Three Treatments for Borderline Personality Disorder: A Multiwave Study," *American Journal of Psychiatry* 164, no. 6 (June 2007): 992–28.

7   J. Feigenbaum, "Dialectical Behavior Therapy: An Increasing Evidence Base," *Journal of Mental Health* (February 2007): 1651–68.

8   Bateman and Krawitz, *Borderline Personality Disorder*, 2, 124–42.

9   Bateman and Krawitz, *Borderline Personality Disorder*, 24.

10   Paul Meier and Robert L. Wise, *Crazy Makers: Getting Along with the Difficult People in Your Life* (Nashville: Thomas Nelson, 2003), 34.

11   Bateman and Krawitz, *Borderline Personality Disorder*, 25.

12   Paul T. Mason and Randi Kreger, *Stop Walking on Eggshells: Taking Your Life Back When Someone You Care about Has Borderline Personality Disorder* (Oakland, CA: New Harbinger, 2010), 25–28.

13   Mason and Kreger, *Stop Walking*, 25–27.

14   Mason and Kreger, *Stop Walking*, 25.

15   Melville, *Breaking Free*, 95.

Chapter Five

1   Paul T. Mason and Randi Kreger, *Stop Walking on Eggshells: Taking Your Life Back When Someone You Care about Has Borderline Personality Disorder* (Oakland, CA: New Harbinger, 2010), 96.

2   Lynn Melville, *Breaking Free from Boomerang Love: Getting Unhooked from Borderline Personality Disorder Relationships* (Santa Maria, CA: Melville Publications, 2009), 41.

3   Mason and Kreger, *Stop Walking*, 119–22.

4   Mason and Kreger, *Stop Walking*, 125–32.

5   M. L. Heldman, *When Words Hurt: How to Keep Criticism from Undermining Your Self-Esteem* (New York: Ballantine, 1990).

Chapter Six

1   Karl Menninger, *The Human Mind* (Garden City, NY: Garden City Publishing, 1930).

2   Kristen Driscoll, "Ruth Bell Graham: A Life Well Lived, Part 2," *Decision Magazine,* June 2013, accessed May 2, 2017, https://billygraham.org/decision-magazine/june-2013/ruth-bell-graham-a-life-well-lived-part-2/.

3   "'Anger' in the KJV Bible," *King James Bible Online,* accessed
     August 29, 2016, https://www.kingjamesbibleonline.org/
     anger/.

4   Institute of Historical Research, "Men and Women: Chal-
     lenging the Stereotypes," *History in Focus: The Victorian
     Era,* accessed August 30, 2016, http://www.history.ac.uk/
     ihr/Focus/Victorians/#menwom.

5   Gary Oliver and H. Norman Wright, *Good Women Get
     Angry: A Woman's Guide to Handling Her Anger, Depression,
     Anxiety, and Stress* (Ann Arbor: Vine Books, 1995).

Chapter Seven

1   Paul Meier and Robert L. Wise, *Crazy Makers: Getting Along
     with the Difficult People in Your Life* (Nashville: Thomas
     Nelson, 2003), 110.

2   Meier and Wise, *Crazy Makers,* 108–9.

3   Meier and Wise, *Crazy Makers,* 107.

4   Katie Howard, "Creating God in Our Own Image,"
     KatieHoward.com, accessed August 30, 2016, http://
     katiehhoward.com/creatinggodinourownimage/.

5   Paul T. Mason and Randi Kreger, *Stop Walking on Eggshells:
     Taking Your Life Back When Someone You Care about Has Bor-
     derline Personality Disorder* (Oakland, CA: New Harbinger,
     2010), 181–84.

Chapter Eight

1   Paul T. Mason and Randi Kreger, *Stop Walking on Eggshells:
     Taking Your Life Back When Someone You Care about*

Has Borderline Personality Disorder (Oakland, CA: New Harbinger, 2010), 111.

2   Nina W. Brown, *Coping with Infuriating, Mean, Critical People: The Destructive Narcissistic Pattern* (Westport, CT: Prager, 2006), 30–50.

3   Margarita Tartakovsky, "How to Help a Loved One with Borderline Personality Disorder, Part 2," PsychCentral, accessed August 31, 2016, https://psychcentral.com/lib/how -to-help-a-loved-one-with-borderline-personality-disorder -part-2/.

4   Melody Beattie, *Codependent No More* (Center City, MN: Hazelden, 1987).

5   Paul Meier and Robert L. Wise, *Crazy Makers: Getting Along with the Difficult People in Your Life* (Nashville: Thomas Nelson, 2003), 179.

Chapter Nine

1   Anthony W. Bateman and Roy Krawitz, *Borderline Personality Disorder: An Evidence-Based Guide for Generalist Mental Health Professionals* (Oxford: Oxford University Press, 2013).

2   Melinda Smith, Lawrence Robinson, and Jeanne Segal, "Helping Someone with Borderline Personality Disorder," Helpguide.org, accessed August 31, 2016, https://www.help guide.org/articles/mental-disorders/helping-someone-with -borderline-personality-disorder.htm?pdf=true.

3   Paul Meier and Robert L. Wise, *Crazy Makers: Getting Along with the Difficult People in Your Life* (Nashville: Thomas Nelson, 2003), 165–66.

4   Lynn Melville, *Breaking Free from Boomerang Love: Getting Unhooked from Borderline Personality Disorder Relationships* (Santa Maria, CA: Melville Publications, 2009), 53.

5   Melville, *Breaking Free,* 187–92.

Chapter Ten

1   Paul Meier and Robert L. Wise, *Crazy Makers: Getting Along with the Difficult People in Your Life* (Nashville: Thomas Nelson, 2003), 21–22.

2   Paul T. Mason and Randi Kreger, *Stop Walking on Eggshells: Taking Your Life Back When Someone You Care about Has Borderline Personality Disorder* (Oakland, CA: New Harbinger, 2010), 87–90.

3   Mason and Kreger, *Stop Walking,* 23–32.

Chapter Eleven

1   Paul Meier and Robert L. Wise, *Crazy Makers: Getting Along with the Difficult People in Your Life* (Nashville: Thomas Nelson, 2003), 116.

2   Paul T. Mason and Randi Kreger, *Stop Walking on Eggshells: Taking Your Life Back When Someone You Care about Has Borderline Personality Disorder* (Oakland, CA: New Harbinger, 2010), 29–32.

3   Melinda Smith, Lawrence Robinson, and Jeanne Segal, "Helping Someone with Borderline Personality Disorder," Helpguide.org, accessed September 2, 2016, https://www

.helpguide.org/articles/mental-disorders/helping-someone -with-borderline-personality-disorder.htm?pdf=true.

4   Margarita Tartakovsky, "How to Help a Loved One with Borderline Personality Disorder, Part 2," PsychCentral, accessed August 30, 2016, https://psychcentral.com/lib/ how-to-help-a-loved-one-with-borderline-personality -disorder-part-2/.

5   Mason and Kreger, *Stop Walking,* 222.

6   Mason and Kreger, *Stop Walking,* 218–19.

Chapter Twelve

1   Paul Meier and Robert L. Wise, *Crazy Makers: Getting Along with the Difficult People in Your Life* (Nashville: Thomas Nelson, 2003), 63–64.

2   American Psychiatric Association, "Practice Guideline for the Treatment of Patients with Borderline Personality Disorder," *American Journal of Psychiatry* 158, no. 10 (Suppl.; October 2001): 1–52.

3   Anthony W. Bateman and Roy Krawitz, *Borderline Personality Disorder: An Evidence-Based Guide for Generalist Mental Health Professionals* (Oxford: Oxford University Press, 2013), 143–46.

Chapter Thirteen

1   Melinda Smith, Lawrence Robinson, and Jeanne Segal, "Helping Someone with Borderline Personality Disorder," Helpguide.org, accessed September 2, 2016, https://www

.helpguide.org/articles/mental-disorders/helping-someone
-with-borderline-personality-disorder.htm?pdf=true.

2   Anthony W. Bateman and Roy Krawitz, *Borderline Personality Disorder: An Evidence-Based Guide for Generalist Mental Health Professionals* (Oxford: Oxford University Press,
2013), 40–41.

3   C. S. Lewis, *The Problem of Pain* (1940; repr., San Francisco: HarperSanFrancisco, 2001), 19.

4   George E. Ganss, *The Spiritual Exercises of Saint Ignatius:
A Translation and Commentary* (Chicago: Loyola Press,
1992).

Suggested Resources

American Psychiatric Association. 2000. *Diagnostic and Statistical Manual of Mental Disorders* (4th ed., text rev.). Washington, DC: American Psychiatric Association.

Bateman, Anthony W., and Roy Krawitz. 2013. *Borderline Personality Disorder: An Evidence-Based Guide for Generalist Mental Health Professionals.* Oxford: Oxford University Press.

Beattoe, M. 1987. *Codependent No More.* Center City, MN: Hazelden.

Bradsjaw, J. 1988. *Healing the Shame That Binds You.* Deerfield Beach, FL: Health Communications.

Brodsky, B., and J. Mann. 1997. "The Biology of the Disorder." *California Alliance for the Mentally Ill Journal* 8:1.

Cauwels, J. 1992. *Imbroglio: Rising to the Challenge of Borderline Personality Disorder.* New York: W. W. Norton.

Engel, B. 1990. *The Emotionally Abused Woman: Overcoming Destructive Patterns and Reclaiming Yourself.* New York: Fawcett Columbine.

Gunderson, J. G. 1984. *Borderline Personality Disorder.* Washington, DC: American Psychiatric Press.

Kreisman, J., and H. Strauss. 1989. *I Hate You—Don't Leave Me.* New York: Avon Books.

Mason, Paul T., and Randi Kreger. 2010. *Stop Walking on Eggshells.* Oakland, CA: New Harbinger.

McGlashan, T. H. 1986. "Long-Term Outcome of Borderline Personalities." The Chestnut Lodge Follow-Up Study. III. *Archives of General Psychiatry* 33:336–340.

Melville, Lynn. 2004. *Breaking Free from Boomerang Love.* Santa Maria, CA: Melville Publications.

Roth, K., and F. B. Friedman. 2003. *Surviving a Borderline Parent.* Oakland, CA: New Harbinger.

Stone, M. H. 1990. *The Fate of Borderline Patients.* New York: Guilford Press.

About New Life Ministries

New Life Ministries, founded by Stephen Arterburn, began in 1988 as New Life Treatment Centers. New Life's nationally broadcast radio program, *New Life Live!*, began in early 1995. The Women of Faith conferences, also founded by Stephen Arterburn, began in 1996. New Life's Counselor Network was formed in 2000, and TV.NewLife .com, the ministry's Internet-based television channel, was launched in 2014. New Life continues to develop and expand their programs and resources to help meet the changing needs of their callers and listeners.

Today, New Life Ministries is a nationally recognized, faith-based broadcasting and counseling nonprofit organization that provides ministry through radio, TV, their counseling network, workshops, and support groups, as well as through their numerous print, audio, and video resources. All New Life resources are based on God's truth and help those who are hurting find and build connections and experience life transformation.

The *New Life Live!* radio program, still the centerpiece of the ministry, is broadcast on Christian radio stations in more than 150 markets. It can also be seen on several network and online channels.

New Life's mission is to reach out compassionately to those seeking emotional and spiritual health and healing for God's glory. New Life Ministries Resource Center receives thousands of calls each month from those looking for help.

For more information, visit newlife.com.

About Stephen Arterburn

Stephen Arterburn, M.Ed., is the founder and chairman of New Life Ministries and host of the number-one nationally syndicated Christian counseling talk show *New Life Live!*, heard and watched by more than two million people each week on nearly two hundred stations nationwide. He is also the host of *New Life TV*, a web-based channel dedicated to transforming lives through God's truth, and he also serves as a teaching pastor in Indianapolis, Indiana.

Stephen is an internationally recognized public speaker and has been featured on national media venues such as *Oprah*, *Inside Edition*, *Good Morning America*, *CNN Live*, and *ABC World News Tonight*; in the *New York Times*, *USA Today*, *US News and World Report*; and even in *GQ* and *Rolling Stone* magazines. Stephen has spoken at major events for the National Center for Fathering, American Association of Christian Counselors, Promise Keepers Canada, the Lifewell Conference in Australia, and the Salvation Army, to name a few.

He is the bestselling author of books such as *Every Man's Battle* and *Healing Is a Choice*. With more than eight million books in print, Stephen has been writing about God's transformational truth since 1984. His ministry focuses on identifying and compassionately responding to the needs of those seeking healing and restoration through God's truth. Along with Dr. Dave Stoop, he edited and produced the number-one-bestselling *Life Recovery Bible*.

Stephen has degrees from Baylor University and the University of North Texas, as well as two honorary doctorates, and is currently completing his doctoral studies in Christian counseling. He resides with his family in Fishers, Indiana.

Stephen Arterburn can be contacted directly at SArterburn@newlife.com.

About Robert Wise

Robert Wise, Ph.D., is an archbishop in the Communion of Evangelical Episcopal Churches, and he has served as principal lecturer for the Bethel Series, teaching in Canada, Germany, and the United States.

In 2014, Pope Francis appointed Robert to be his Apostolic Representative for Christian Unity. While working around the world, he has helped plant churches in Canada, England, and the United States.

Robert is the author of numerous articles and thirty-four published books, which have been translated into multiple languages, including Spanish, Dutch, Chinese, Japanese, and German.

In his nonfiction works, Robert has often addressed issues of struggle. His book *When There Is No Miracle*, a survey of why innocent people struggle with pain, has sold for more than forty years, and he authored *When the Night Is Too Long* as its sequel.

Windows of the Soul describes how God uses our dreams as a means for spiritual growth. In *Spiritual Abundance*, he explores the insights of the early church fathers of the first five centuries to discover their directives for personal growth.

More recently, Robert wrote *Fearless for Life*, covering how Christians can overcome fear with the power of faith in their lives. *Crazy Makers* presents techniques for dealing with difficult and narcissistic persons. And in 2013, his book *Crossing the Threshold of Eternity: What the Dying Can Teach the Living* was published.

At David C Cook, we equip the local church around
the corner and around the globe to make disciples.
Come see how we are working together—go to
www.davidccook.com. Thank you!

transforming lives together